Australian Biographical Monographs

9

Australian Biographical Monographs
Series Editor: Scott Prasser

Previous Volumes

1	*Joseph Lyons* *and the Management of Adversity*	Kevin Andrews
2	*Harold Holt* *and the Liberal Imagination*	Tom Frame
3	*Johannes Bjelke-Petersen*	Bruce Kingston
4	*Lindsay Thompson* *Character, Competence and Conviction*	William Westerman
5	*Neville Wran*	David Clune
6	*Robert Menzies* *Man or Myth*	Scott Prasser
7	*Stanley Melbourne Bruce* *Institution Builder*	David Lee
8	*John Grey Gorton* *Australian to the Bootheels:* *The paradoxical life of Gorton*	Paul Williams

Australian Biographical Monographs

9

Sir Robert Askin

Paul Loughnan

Connor Court Publishing

Published in 2020 by Connor Court Publishing Pty Ltd

Copyright © Paul Loughnan 2020

All rights reserved. No part of this book may be reproduced or transmitted in any form or by any means, electronic or mechanical, including photo copying, recording or by any information storage and retrieval system, without prior permission in writing from the publisher.

Connor Court Publishing Pty Ltd
PO Box 7257
Redland Bay QLD 4165
sales@connorcourt.com
www.connorcourt.com
Phone 0497-900-685

Printed in Australia

ISBN: 9781922449368

Front cover design: Maria Giordano

Front cover picture: Wikipedia Commons.

This monograph is dedicated to Kate, Anthony, Ben, Lilly and Amelia

"I didn't have any particular educational qualifications or any other outstanding attributes in my opinion, but I was a good mixer. I understood people and understood what made the bulk of them tick and what they hoped for. I think I understood that and addressed my policies accordingly."

Source: Pratt, Mel, Interview with Sir Robert Askin, former Premier of NSW, sound recording and transcript, October 7-11, 1976, Canberra, National Library of Australia, 1976

Acknowledgements

I would like to acknowledge Dr Scott Prasser for his insightful and dedicated editorship. Many thanks also to Dr Graeme Starr who was there at the time and who's first-hand knowledge of Askin has brought additional insights to my original research. I also acknowledge the late Dr Mark Hayne who was my first lecturer at the University of New England (UNE) and rekindled my interest in history.

The debt to my post-graduate supervisors is immense. Thanks to Professor Frank Bongiorno of the Australian National University and Dr Tim Battin of UNE for their sage advice and inspiration which culminated in the completion of the doctoral degree which made this monograph possible.

Australian Biographical Monographs

Series overview

The Connor Court Publishing's Australian Biographical Series on past leading Australian political leaders and other important figures seeks to provide an overview for those who are unfamiliar with the subject and to highlight the person's particular importance, controversies and contributions to Australia's progress.

The monographs are scholarly rather than academic in focus placing emphasis on a clear narrative, but with careful attention to referencing to ensure views expressed are supported by appropriate sources and evidence.

The Series was initiated because of the decline in the study of Australian history at our schools and universities and the consequential lack of knowledge or even worse, distorted views of some of Australia's leading figures who deserve to be remembered, understood for both their achievements, and as each volume also highlights, their flaws.

Sir Robert Askin, Liberal Premier of New South Wales

from 1965 to 1975, was the longest serving and most successful Liberal Premier winning four elections in a row and who retired at a time of his own choosing. He came from a modest but happy family background, won a state bursary to secondary college, enlisted in the Australian Imperial Force and served in New Guinea. He was a natural for politics – he liked people, fellowship, was a good judge of character, and given his background, understood the real needs of the general public. Unfortunately, Askin's reputation has been overshadowed by long standing allegations of corruption.

This monograph by Dr Paul Loughnan based on his extensive research for his doctorate on Askin, sets the record straight. Paul's youth was bookended by Askin's 1965-75 premiership which ignited his interest in Sir Robert and his government. This monograph informs us about Askin's character and achievements, but more importantly, demolishes once and for all the myths concerning his alleged corruption. They are just not true. So, this monograph allows us to see Askin for the first time for what he really was – a great leader, an astute pragmatic politician who steered his party to successes which have not been matched since.

Author's Preface

The research for this biographical monograph is primarily drawn from my PhD dissertation, *A History of the Askin Government 1965-1975* awarded by the University of New England (Faculty of Humanities, Arts, Social Sciences and Education) in 2014. As a student of history, despite my human flaws and failings, neutrality and non-partisanship are my objectives. However, there is a caveat: I am fond of, The Australian Labor Party and the Liberal-National Party Coalition equally, and the contribution of the other parties and independents that come and go, in our great Australian democracy. I also must confess that I am a tragic 'swinging voter'.

Introduction

On 14 September 1981, when over a thousand invited mourners left Sir Robert Askin's state funeral at St Andrew's Cathedral in Sydney with "Onward Christian Soldiers" still ringing in their ears, they were greeted by the headline in the *National Times* at the nearby news stand, "ASKIN: FRIEND TO ORGANISED CRIME".[1] It was claimed by the young journalist David Hickie that Askin and Police Commissioner Hanson, were each paid $100,000 per year from 1967-8 until Askin's retirement in 1975 to allow Perce Galea to operate his illegal casino with impunity. It was extraordinary that this claim was based on an anonymous so called "impeccable source".[2] Galea was a "major [Sydney] crime figure," who "laundered large amounts of drug money".[3] Casinos were not legalised in New South Wales (NSW) until 1992.

The article in the *National Times* owned by John Fairfax and Sons was the genesis of the Askin corruption myth which became 'received wisdom.' As a result, most people over the age of fifty-five often identify Askin as a corrupt premier which is usually followed by an unsupported and far-fetched story. In the public domain the received wisdom has sometimes provided fertile ground for unsubstantiated allegations to be revived to facilitate numerous agendas. For example, the renowned journalist Kate McClymont, who according to David Marr is the "investigative journalist's investigative journalist," penned an article in the *Sydney Morning Herald* (*SMH*) on 28 July 2008, which begins with "The disgraced former Liberal Premier Bob Askin." Why disgraced? Because of one article published in 1981, edited by David Marr who refuses to engage in the topic every time corroborated and substantiated evidence is mentioned.

This became clear to the author when the research for the Askin project began. A taxi driver told me that Bob Askin was a crook. But it turned out that he had not emigrated from the United Kingdom at the time of the incident he had recalled and at that time Askin was dead. Nonetheless, he was adamant. Another time a very excited and genuinely interested woman came bounding up to me at the NSW archives and told me that her father used to have a dental practice in Macquarie Street and Bob Askin had been one of his patients. There had been too many implausible stories. And I was 'fed up' so I said, "don't tell me, Askin thieved gold fillings out of people's mouths while they were sleeping and tried to flog them to your father." I thought why not? He had been accused of everything else. Fortunately, she was amused, and appreciated the sense of the ridiculous.

The research for this biographical monograph is primarily drawn from my PhD dissertation, *A History of the Askin Government 1965-1975*, awarded by the University of New England (Faculty of Humanities, Arts, Social Sciences and Education) in 2014. The principal argument of the dissertation is that Askin's contribution as leader was crucial to the electoral success and longevity of the Liberal-Country Party Coalition government in New South Wales (NSW). But this monograph is the story of Bob Askin: From humble beginnings, to become the first citizen of the state of NSW. It is a story of a commendable life in public service, but also an account of how easily reputations can be distorted by political myths and mischief.

It will be clearly demonstrated that the Askin corruption myth was based on unsubstantiated and uncorroborated allegations. The conclusion was reached after rigorous research including discourse with David Hickie, the young journalist, and David Marr, the editor of the *National Times* in 1981. These reported allegations were a symptom of 'starry eyed and bushy tailed' inexperienced journalism. It was revealed in the book *Heralds and Angles: The House of Fairfax*, authored by Gavin Souter, who was the company's historian, that the publication was a result of the untrained and inexperienced editorship on the part of David Marr. It is noteworthy that Marr has not held a position as editor since the Askin debacle.

It is a travesty that the corruption myth took on a life of its own at the expense of the credibility of Askin's premiership. In May 1965 Askin was elected Premier of NSW. He led the Liberal-Country Party Coalition until he chose to retire in 1975. Prior to this, the Liberals had languished in opposition for twenty-four years and it appeared that they were doomed to become a "permanent opposition" party.[4] This was an extraordinary feat in the context of 'swinging 60s.' The coming of age of the 'baby boomers,' 'the times they are a changing,' the sexual revolution, long hair, anti-Vietnam war demonstrations; the era was defined by modern music immortalised by Janis Joplin, Jimmy Hendrix, Bob Dylan and Joan Baez to name but a few, who were in stark contrast to the crooners of the 1940s-50s. This was sometimes an antithesis to the traditional way of life of the war time and post-war boom generation. It was coined the 'generation gap.'

Askin's extraordinary record as the longest serving and most politically successful NSW Liberal Premier, deserves much more respect than it has received, even from his own party.[5] Along with Sir Robert Menzies, the former Australian Prime Minster, and the Victorian Premier, Sir Henry Bolte, and more recently Mike Baird, the former NSW Premier, Askin is one of the few politicians to exit from the leadership of a Liberal government at the time of his own choosing. However, soon after Askin's resignation the Liberals returned to the opposition benches until 1988. Before the O'Farrell Coalition Government was elected in 2011 the Liberal Party had held office in NSW for only 18 years since the Second World War.

Early formative years

Robin William Askin was born on 4 April 1907 at Sydney Women's Hospital in Crown Street Sydney and was the illegitimate son of the widow Laura Halliday née Rowe. (Askin disliked his first name and changed it to Robert in 1971; he was known as Robert or Bob or only very occasionally as Rob). Ellen produced two more sons with Askin's father, William James Askin, and later married in September 1916. The *Legitimation Act 1902* enabled parents to re-register the birth of an illegitimate child: William Askin re-registered Robin Askin's birth on 26 September 1916.[6]

In Australian society until the 1960s, unsanctioned sexual acts created moral outrage and the child of such a union was branded with the stigma of illegitimacy.[7] The child had no right to the name of the mother or the father and no status as a legitimate member of society.[8] This might explain why Askin was reticent regarding the circumstances of his birth in his posterity interview in 1976. He merely stated, "My mother met my father and I was born in Sydney".[9]

By the time Askin's parents took up together, the family's financial circumstances had been reduced. Askin's grandfather had owned a small shipping company at Semaphore, South Australia and captained several vessels including the *Falls of Dee*, *Marianna* and *Bittern*. Askin's father had been employed by the company but after the advent of steam power, the sailing vessels were superseded, and his father was made redundant.[10]

After Askin was born his father gained employment as a porter on the NSW State Railway. The family relocated to Stuart Town in the central west of NSW, which was Askin's mother's hometown. The young Askin, who was affectionately known as "Billy," experienced country life, commenced his schooling and thrived amongst his large, extended family.[11]

The railway job required Askin's father to be away from the family for extended periods, so he changed jobs and began to work for the tramway service in Sydney.[12] The family moved to the inner-city suburb of Glebe, where Askin attended the infants section of the Forest Lodge Public School and finished his primary school education at Glebe Public School.[13] Askin lived in Glebe with his parents until he was 29. All indications are that family life was important to the Askins.

In the early decades of the 20th century, Glebe was a unique, socially diverse local community. It stretched from the salubrious harbour front area of Glebe Point to the zone between Glebe Point, the areas north of Parramatta Road and Broadway where Askin lived. This area was occupied by a mixture of salary-earning middle class and working class citizens. The Broadway area was inhabited by labourers and disposed people on the fringe of society.[14]

When Askin became a Member of the Legislative Assembly (MLA) he was renowned for his ability to communicate with people across the whole spectrum of society. Growing up in a lively and diverse community such as Glebe would no doubt have assisted Askin in acquiring these skills. He capitalised on his own working-class roots when he was courting the working class such as railway workers who were traditional Labor voters. Askin, the consummate raconteur, was able to tell the story of how his family was evicted from their home at Glebe after his father lost his job due to the railway strike of 1917 and he slept the night with his father in Wentworth Park.[15]

There is no doubt that Askin possessed a very good intellect. In 1919 after he had completed his six years of primary school, he was awarded a state bursary which was based on scholastic merit. The bursary gained him admission to the Sydney Technical High School, an academically selective institution located in Ultimo.[16] Sydney Technical High School was within an easy walking distance from Askin's home in Glebe. The boy's school provided a general and technical education for future "managers or masters, foreman or overseers and future captains of industry".[17] When Askin returned to his alma mater in 1969 to unveil the plaque in honour of the famous aviator Sir Charles Kingsford Smith, who had attended the school in 1912, he was introduced by the head master as the first citizen of the state.[18] He retained good memories of his school days and of class-mates, but it is ironic, that because of the corruption myth, there are no plaques anywhere in recognition of Askin's life or his public service.

After young Askin completed the Intermediate Certificate in 1922, he began an apprenticeship as an electrician. After almost electrocuting his employer, Askin's father was informed that the young man had talent but not in the electrical trade.[19] William then made a successful application for his son to join the NSW Government's Savings Bank in Martin Place in 1922.[20] Askin worked as a junior clerk until 1928 when he was promoted to work in the records department where he stayed until 1931.

Askin, like most Australians, was affected by the Great Depression of the 1930s. In 1931 there was a run on the NSW Savings Bank and the bank could not meet its at-call demands.[21] Due to the financial problems of the bank, Askin worked "one day on and one day off". During this period, he engaged in odd jobs and "did a lot of reading to improve (himself)". His main interests were autobiographies, biographies, history, economics and politics.

Askin was an avid joiner. He joined the first division of the Glebe football league in 1928 and he was hooker for the reserve grade. In 1934 he was Vice-Captain of the Rural Bank's premiership team.[22] He joined a debating club, a rifle club, and served on the executive of the NSW Swimming Association from 1934 to 1939. He also served as Vice-President from 1939-40 and President from 1940-41 of the Rural Bank's branch of the United Bank Officers' Association.[23] This experience would have helped him fulfil his later acquired political aspirations.

Askin's wife was unswerving in her support for his political aspirations. Askin married Mollie Isabelle Underhill at the Methodist Church at Gilbert Park in Manly on 5 February 1937.[24] Mollie was from a well-to-do middle-class family from Bega on the South Coast of NSW. She worked with Askin at the bank as a typist and her father was secretary of The Associated Racing Clubs. Mollie was elegant, well-educated and a champion swimmer at the Manly Swimming Club. They made their home in Manly and remained there for the rest of their lives.[25]

On 30 March 1942, Askin enlisted in the Australian Imperial Force (AIF) when he was 35 years of age.[26] His comrades referred to his cohort as the "old and the bold".[27] In November 1942 he joined the 2/31st Battalion in Papua for two months, then in New Guinea, until July 1945 when he landed in Balikpapan, Borneo where he was promoted to Sergeant under the command of Lieutenant Colonel Murray Robson.[28]

Askin used his banking experience and managed the Battalion accounts and canteen and mess funds; he was also the SP bookmaker for the Battalion. His oratorical skill came to the fore when he organised a debate to entertain the 'diggers'. Robson, who was on leave from his duties as the MLA for the seat of Vaucluse in the NSW Parliament, was impressed with Askin and told him to make contact after the war if he was interested in a political career.[29]

After the War, Askin had a chance meeting with Murray Robson in a Sydney street.[30] He was clearly not a person to overlook his chances. After a yarn and a beer, which could be construed as a defining moment for Askin, Robson recruited him to assist in his 1947 election campaign for his seat of Vaucluse. After Robson's campaign, Askin's appetite for politics had been whetted so he paid his membership fee and joined the Manly branch of the Liberal Party. After about a year as an active member of the Manly branch he was elected president. Askin also became President of the Mackellar Federal Electoral Conference and managed the successful campaign of Bill Wentworth who won Mackellar at the 1949 federal election.[31]

Before the 1950 NSW State election, there was a redistribution of boundaries in the Northern Beaches area of Sydney due to the expanding population. The new seat of Collaroy was created, which incorporated part of Manly and stretched to Palm Beach in the north. It was clearly a good, winnable and safe seat for a youngish war veteran who by that time was reasonably well politically connected and becoming entrenched in the community. Askin nominated for the pre-selection and won in the first ballot. At 43 years of age, he gained the safe seat of Collaroy in the 1950 election, with a 63 per cent majority of the primary vote against a good field of candidates.[32]

Askin's path to the leadership of the Liberal Party

When Askin became the new MLA for Collaroy he was cut from a very different cloth from his counterparts in the Parliamentary Liberal Party. There were sixteen new MLA Liberals between 1947 and 1953 and Askin was one of three who came from a working class background (based on the occupation of the member's father).[33] Askin was also in the one third-minority of Liberal members from 1945 to 1962 who were full-time members. During this period, the majority of members participated in parliament on a part-time basis, often taking second place to their involvement in outside business interests.[34] But for Askin, politics took second place to nothing. He entered parliament with no conflicting outside interests, unlike most Liberal members at the time, but he took with him a degree of ambition that was soon to be rewarded with a rapid rise to leadership.

During his first term in the parliament, Askin was serving his 'apprenticeship' and was rarely in the spotlight. But he was assiduous in his activities in support of those issues which he detected as being keys to the interests of his constituents in Collaroy, such as the need for improved public transport to the Northern Beaches and an increase in the pension and superannuation fund for government employees.[35] As Askin's first term progressed he found his home in the NSW Parliament and began to flourish in the robust adversarial environment of the 'bear pit'. His diligent performance was recognised in 1954 when he was elected deputy leader after only four years in the parliament.

After the 1953 landslide loss to the incumbent Labor Government, the Liberal Party was deeply divided. Between 1954 and 1959 there were four leaders of the parliamentary party. It had split into two groups, one led by Philip (Pat) Morton and the other led by former leader Vernon Treatt. These were fluid and informal groups, not based on ideological factions, but the simpler issue of leadership and the practical question of who could lead the Liberals to electoral success. Turmoil over leadership contributed significantly to the electoral defeat of the Liberals in 1959.

In the wake of this election defeat of the Liberals Askin saw his opportunity and seized the leadership. His leadership skills had served him well and, as deputy he had worked hard to establish and preserve his position of authority. Despite his wheeling and dealing behind the scenes in the leadership intrigues, Askin was always aware of the need to retain the favour of his peers and remain onside with all his parliamentary colleagues in both groups. Equally, his advocacy for the salary-earning middle-class voter reflected his understanding of the need to retain the favour of constituents. The fact that he was the only Liberal member to increase his majority in the 1953 election and continue to grow this lead through to the 1959 election further exemplifies this point. Moreover, he was able to convince his peers to recognise that he had political coattails and that his acceptance in the electorate as an attractive candidate could develop into support for the wider Liberal Party as a potential election winner. Askin played his hand well. His preference for logistics over strategy enabled him to wait until he could stand for the leadership unopposed. Following a lengthy debate in the party room, Morton was persuaded to resign and Askin was elected unanimously as leader of the parliamentary Liberal Party.

Askin as leader

Bob Askin was not the sort of politician who was ever likely to write very much that would reveal a deep and defined political philosophy. Graeme Starr, who worked with Askin in developing policy for the successful 1965 election, described his philosophy as being much the same as that of George Washington Plunkitt: "of an exceedin' accommodatin' character".[36] Nevertheless, Askin made his views on leadership clear to the Parliament as early as 1954 when he became deputy leader and stressed his belief that, once elected, a Liberal leader must be allowed to lead: differences of opinion among members should "all be thrashed out honestly and openly and settled" and the members should remain "all united, without exception, in support of our present leader"[37] until he announces his intention to resign.

Upon his election as leader in 1959, Askin presided

over a transition in the Liberal Party and in its public image.[38] He had some good fortune in that the prestige of his position was enhanced by an Opposition victory in a State referendum in 1961, enabling Askin to assert his authority in a manner neglected by his predecessors. In endeavouring to push his party towards new goals he provided its first experience of dynamic leadership. As a new leader, however, Askin was also confronted with many early challenges. The Liberal Party was despondent, divided and in desperate need of reinvention and unification. The relationship with the Country Party was tenuous while that with the organisational wing of the Liberal Party was initially difficult and sometimes even acrimonious.[39] Askin also needed to maintain his authority over the parliamentary party. Each of these three relationships had the capacity to undermine the new leader's position and to challenge any hope he had of winning government. Each called for sensitive handling, and each required a great deal of time.

Time was one thing that Askin clearly had in abundance as a new leader with three years to wait for the next election – and perhaps six years before there was any realistic hope of winning government. Askin used his time well. He quickly sorted out any of the difficulties his party had with the Country Party (coalition relations are always problematic in opposition) and settled on a sound working arrangement with that party's talented leader Charles Cutler. Similarly, with his experience as deputy to his three predecessors, he soon mastered the parliamentary party. His initial failure to understand the importance of the relationship with the Liberal Party organisation, however, probably contributed significantly to his electoral defeat in 1962, but taught him a lesson that was to bring him and his party their greatest ever success in 1965.

A review of Askin's time as leader suggests that he was instinctively and acutely aware of four key ingredients for successful political leadership: insight and adaptability to changing political circumstances; maintaining the authority to lead; the requirement to focus on the needs of voters; and awareness of the needs of peers.[40] Askin's instincts were sharp, as demonstrated by his mastery of these basic, but essential tenets, which enabled him to hold power until he chose to retire. He quickly revealed that, along with his inherent political talents, he was a 'learning leader' and he worked assiduously at developing his leadership skills, apparently very conscious of the need to eliminate all potential challenges. It is worth examining how Askin mixed the four 'key ingredients' that enabled him to maintain stable leadership in a party where such stability had plainly been so sadly lacking.

Awareness of the needs of peers

The unanimity of his election as leader in 1959 and the established principle in the party to trust the leader with unimpeded authority to select his own ministers or shadows enabled Askin to settle down any tension in the Parliamentary Liberal Party. There were, of course, other younger and equally ambitious Members, notably Tom Lewis and Eric Willis, who each in turn, was to succeed Askin after he retired. Both were known to harbour long-term leadership aspirations, so it was necessary for Askin to eliminate any machinations. Political leaders in the Australian parliamentary system are as likely to be deposed by their own party as they are by the electorate. Askin drew Tom Lewis into his orbit where, under his watchful eye, Lewis "became his friend, drinking mate and supporter".[41] Askin allocated relatively junior portfolios to Lewis, despite his ability as a minister. Lewis enjoyed and courted the media: he was a 'show pony' and Askin had his measure. Askin's rationale was to retard Lewis's media profile by keeping him away from the metropolitan area. Askin was probably not overly concerned when as Minister for Lands his "drinking mate" was required to oversee the construction of the dingo fence in outback NSW. Lewis found that Askin was "one of the shrewdest politicians you could ever meet".[42]

Askin's judgement of Lewis was 'right on the money.' In late 1971 after Askin's second heart attack, speculation was rife about his retirement. True to form, Lewis was first out of the stalls. It was tulip time at Moss Vale where he lived, and he invited all the state Liberal politicians to a barbeque at his home to garner their support. When the ALP learned of the possible leadership tussle they could not contain their amusement. When they passed Coalition members in the corridors of Parliament House they felt compelled to whistle, hum or sing 'tip toe through the tulips,' much to the chagrin of the government members.[43] Askin did not choose to retire, which left Lewis trudging through the tulips for the next three years.

Eric Willis was elected deputy leader in 1959 at the same time Askin became leader and was considered the heir apparent to the leadership. By 1965 when the Askin Government was first elected, Willis had proven to be a very capable and loyal deputy and did not pose a threat to Askin's leadership. In contrast to his strategy with Lewis, Askin utilised Willis's talents and appointed him Minister for Labour and Industry, Chief Secretary and Minister for Tourist Activities. Askin's judgement proved to be accurate, and Willis remained his loyal deputy until Askin retired in 1975.

There was a third potential leadership aspirant in the form of John Maddison, an able, popular and politically attractive parliamentarian admired by the party organisation. Askin did not feel directly threatened by Maddison, but he had to make sure that his ability and intelligence were harnessed. Askin appointed him Minister for Justice in 1965 and rewarded him with the

Police Ministry in 1973.[44] Maddison was a lawyer by profession and was invaluable in legislating the State Superannuation Scheme, Law Reform Commission and other law reforms outlined in the four election policies.

Askin used his senior members like former leader Pat Morton and Kevin Ellis with skill. Morton, for example, still a potential leadership rival, was appointed to the senior position as Minister for Local Government and Highways, an important and politically sensitive position held in the previous government by the Deputy Premier. Ellis did not harbour any leadership ambitions but there was some feeling that his independent character would be a destabilising influence in the cabinet. He was idealistic, which put his temperament at odds with Askin, and so to avoid constant disagreement in the cabinet, Askin offered him the position of speaker. Ellis accepted and he held the position with some distinction from 1965 to 1973.

Askin's skilful management of cabinet was best demonstrated by his relations with his younger, respected, and more able ministers, most notably Wal Fife and Milton Morris. He granted his ministers full autonomy. According to Fife, a longstanding member of Askin's cabinet: "when dealing with a minister, Askin left them alone. He did not look over their shoulders. He knew three or four things in each Department that were possibly sensitive".[45] Davis Hughes, Askin's

Minister for Public Works, made much the same point when he said several years later to Fife: "I give Askin an A+ for leadership. Not once did he interfere with anything I was actually doing at the Opera House".[46] Another Country Party Minister, Fuller, recalled that he enjoyed full autonomy in administering his portfolio, but he stated that "you would soon get a phone call over a contentious issue".[47]

Milton Morris, the Minister for Transport throughout the entire Askin Government, echoed this point:

> I became concerned at one point about my lack of contact with Askin and rang the Premier and said to him 'Outside of Cabinet meetings, I have not spoken with you for three months.'. To this he replied, 'Milton that makes you top of the pops. By comparison I have some Ministers running into my office every few days asking for advice. If I have some advice for you, I will call you. Otherwise you should be confident that I am happy with the way you are running things.[48]

Maintaining leadership authority

Leadership of the parliamentary Liberal Party, especially in New South Wales, involves more than simply being the elected leader of a group of politicians. The elected leader must be patient and a cooperative member of the leadership of the Liberal Party organisation. It is imperative that the leader demonstrates that he is the leader of the government with responsibilities to the whole state and not just his own faction, party or the Coalition. A leader's authority can be judged by how well he handles all these facets of leadership.[49]

The foundation for Askin's premiership was built on his capacity to reunify his party and build a strong and durable relationship with the Country Party. This mammoth task had eluded all his Liberal predecessors and demonstrated his understanding and his natural preference for co-operation. These harmonious relationships were fundamental to Askin's success.

Charles Cutler was elected leader of the Country Party during the same period as Askin in 1959. The two leaders were "made for each other" which was essential to the success of the Coalition.[50] Certainly Askin's very social temperament was susceptible to such a relationship. Cutler was an enlivening and sociable character who, like Askin, enjoyed a "beer and a bet".[51] As Fuller, the Country Party member and Minister for Decentralisation commented, "the number of barrels of beer Charlie Cutler and Askin drank nobody would know".[52]

Both leaders were pragmatic and realised that the unity of their parties was essential in order to break Labor's stranglehold in NSW. The 1962 election campaign proved to be a dress rehearsal for the successful campaign of 1965. The Liberal Party and Country Party had presented a united front and it was agreed that a joint policy speech would improve the electoral prospects of both parties at the next election.[53] Equally important, the difficult question over triangular contests for country seats was settled, largely as a result of Askin's growing recognition of the expertise of his organisational leaders like General Secretary John Carrick and successive State Presidents, Bob Cotton, Ralph Honner and Jock Pagan, all of whom took a practical approach to working out mutually acceptable arrangements with the Country Party organisation.

This patching up of the relationship between the parliamentary leader and the key organisational and secretariat leaders came to be a major factor in the maintenance of stability of the government for over a decade. This showed up most clearly after the unsuccessful 1962 election, prior to which Askin kept the organisation at arm's length on policy-development questions. He did not repeat his mistake. After 1962, Askin and Carrick decided to restore the role of the joint policy committee which had first been provided for in the earliest days of the party. A research officer, Graeme Starr, was appointed to manage the committee, which was chaired by Askin and included the State President, six other senior members of the State Executive, and seven members of the shadow cabinet appointed by the leader. The parliamentarians appointed by Askin were Eric Willis, Wal Fife, Dick Healy, Harry Jago, Ken McCaw, John Maddison and Milton Morris, all people who were soon to become senior ministers and who had deep roots in and commitments to the Liberal Party as a political organisation. Starr points out that the full policy committee met "religiously" every month in the two years leading up to the 1965 election, with other shadow ministers attending from time to time so that all significant areas of policy were thoroughly examined.[54] While Askin remained the driver of all policy, all decisions received the consensual approval of the senior parliamentary and organisational leaders of the party, thus further reinforcing the authority of the leader.

Similarly, Askin's skills as a leader of government became apparent to most people when he attended the Premiers' Conference in Canberra barely two weeks after the 1965 election. As premier of the senior state it was Askin's task to speak first and to outline the financial case and expectations of the states. Askin was praised in the lobbies of Parliament House for his success in handling his first Premiers' Conference.[55] After Askin reported to the Cabinet on the outcome of the Premiers' Conference and the Loans Council, the ministers expressed their thanks and placed on the record that they were "greatly impressed with the very effective way in which the Premier and the Deputy Premier had represented NSW in the meeting".[56] As for the electorate, there was wide and consistent press coverage that argued he had got the best loan deal of any state. After Askin's first Premiers' Conference in 1965, he evolved into a formidable warrior in his quest for a more equitable share of Commonwealth revenue. Headlines such as "NSW best of loan allocations"[57] certainly demonstrated to the electorate that he was diligent in his efforts.

Insight and adaptability

Askin learned quickly from his first Premiers' Conference that he could act unilaterally against his fellow premiers to cut a deal that would benefit New South Wales. This helped transform him into an imposing figure on the national stage. He also quickly recognised that he could blame the Commonwealth in instances where he had to break election promises if those promises were underpinned by federal funding. For example, in 1969 Askin blamed the Gorton Government for the increase in the states' taxes and charges and highlighted the tight rein that the Commonwealth held on the states in regard to where the Commonwealth grants were spent.[58] Similarly in the lead-up to the 1972 federal election, Askin threatened to increase taxes and charges in the August budget and blame it on the "dithering" McMahon Government.[59] Later in 1973 after the Whitlam Labor Government was elected, Askin was able to claim take the 'lion's share' of grants earmarked for decentralisation initiatives which included Whitlam's pet project, the Albury-Wodonga growth centre.[60]

State aid to independent schools was one of the major policy issues that confronted Askin. It was a perennial issue and was arguably the most contentious political controversy of the 1960s. Despite support for state aid from the Country Party, support in the Liberal Party was far from unanimous and there was some very bitter opposition to it in both the parliamentary and the organisational wings of the party. There were even loud calls for the sacking of the NSW Liberal Party General Secretary, John Carrick, who championed state aid both because he regarded it as right in principle and because he saw it as a means of expanding the party base.[61] The party organisation finally came around to supporting state aid, against the opposition of a small, but noisy minority on the State Executive, but the division was sufficient to sway a majority of the parliamentary party in 1962 and the issue was not pursued by Askin at this time. Thus, the chance to embrace a major policy initiative was missed and all that Askin was able to promise at the election in 1962 was free bus travel for all school children and increased bursaries for non-government as well as government schools.[62] These were certainly popular initiatives, but they were really little more than gestures in the state aid debate.

The dithering on the state aid issue alone might well have been enough to explain the 1962 electoral defeat. The failure to act decisively was another mistake by Askin, but he made it clear that he would adapt to the new realities on the issue and not make the same mistake again. By the time of the 1965 election Askin had moved the issue through his policy committee and he asserted that the times demanded a positive approach and a settlement of the state aid issue. Askin was not yet fully convinced that the issue was necessarily a vote-winner, but he was persuaded by Carrick and others (including Prime Minister Sir Robert Menzies who had introduced it federally in 1963) that state aid was right in principle. The voters agreed in 1965 and in subsequent elections. When the 1968 election came around, Askin was able to say with some pride that "aid to independent schools is now a generally accepted principle".[63]

Askin rarely allowed hubris to undermine his proven art of politics, however this was not the case in 1970 with the law and order issue. The 'times were a changing' and the baby boomers were coming of age and Askin was seemingly out of touch. To the backdrop of the anti-Vietnam War Moratorium marches which started in May 1970, Askin backed conservativism over pragmatism with the controversial *Summary Offences Bill* which blatantly attempted to stifle the protests.

The political test for this came quickly in September with the Georges River by-election. The by-election was a disaster for the Government and Askin was out-campaigned by the young Frank Walker and the ALP. The Georges River electorate was considered a 'fairly representative seat' of the state. The ALP campaigned on the bread and butter issues of cost of living and education, ignoring the issue of law and order. The issue appears to have had little appeal to voters in a State by-election, perhaps because many of the voters would probably have been parents and grandparents of the demonstrators or even demonstrators themselves. The ALP easily won the seat with a huge 9 per cent swing. Despite this major blunder in judgement, Askin persisted with a watered-down *Summary Offences Bill* and was punished at the state election in 1971 from which the Coalition emerged with a significantly reduced majority.[64]

Focus on the needs of voters

Askin's focus on the interests of the voters was the source of a running routine at meetings of his policy committee. It was a routine that was something more than a joke. Following an hour or more of analysis and debate on the pros and cons of a detailed policy recommendation, Askin would cut to the threshold question: "Right, now where are the votes?"[65] It was far from being the only question that mattered to Askin, but it was one that he was never prepared to overlook.

Aside from a few misjudgements on policy such as his handling of the state aid in his early months as leader and rather obstinate position on the *Summary Offences Bill*, Askin's ability to relate to voters and understand the needs of the electorate was exceptional. This had been obvious to any serious observer from the start of his time as leader, but particularly so as he progressed from his 1965 state election campaign. In fact, it was really evident from the start of his political career. In 1950, for example, when he first sought preselection by the Liberal Party, he came with little political experience other than that gained in the Bank Officers' Association and with a background that was described as "27 years of insulated conformity as a minor official of the Rural

Bank".[66] Nevertheless, he ran against a strong field of good candidates to win the party's nomination for the safe seat of Collaroy, largely because this 'insulation' never undermined his instincts about what the voters (or, in this case, the preselectors) need.

Askin's maiden speech in the NSW Parliament on 20 September 1950 was based on his empathy with the wage-earning voters who were fundamental to his gaining the deputy leadership in 1954, the leadership of his party in 1959, and the premiership in 1965. Askin was able to engage with these voters because he was one of them. He spoke from the people rather than to them when he addressed the basic amenity of sewerage, education facilities, transport, and housing, the plight of the housewife, inflation, federal-state relations and the NSW Surf Life Saving Association.

Equally significantly, Askin courted the traditional Labor supporters such as railway workers, public servants, pensioners and retired public servants who were struggling under the pressures of inflation. He was perceived as being able to relate to "the language of the ordinary working man" and wherever he went, whether it be the football, a pub or an official function everybody was a potential vote and he made a point of speaking to everyone.[67]

The effects of the character and style of Askin's relations with the public were reflected in a succession of election results. His first election as leader, the 1962 campaign, may have been unsuccessful, but it provided the opportunity for the Liberals to display a style of leadership that could be perfected over the following three years to take them to government in 1965. This style of leadership (Askin's style) was summarised in a popular news magazine article soon after Askin became premier, noting that it involved giving the Liberals "a fresh Leftward look" and a purging of the 'old guard,' so that after 1962 the more traditional elements of the Liberal Party had been replaced by younger and more enthusiastic members eager to follow Askin's leadership (thus ensuring Askin much more authority than his predecessors).[68] It also underscored the image of a more innovative party willing to focus on the needs of voters and remain more responsive to public interests.

In the 1968 election, the major issues were housing, education, support for all rural communities in the wake of the drought, and family benefits.[69] Askin leveraged his newly minted Premiers' Conference skills and garnered the 'lion's share' of Commonwealth funds.[70] The largesse this permitted gilded the pathway for Askin's success in the election on 24 February 1968 with an increased majority.

As mentioned above, in 1971 Askin made a rare detour from his voter savvy playbook. He allowed himself to get too caught up with conservatism in the form of the *Summary Offences Act* rather follow the pulse of the electorate and it nearly cost him his premiership. In 1973 Askin redeemed himself. He called an early election to capitalise on the massive fall in popularity of the Whitlam Government.[71] Askin hammered the issues of record high inflation and even blamed the union-affiliated-ALP for increased industrial unrest which was plaguing NSW.[72]

Despite the dull 1973 election, a moment of light relief was captured when Whitlam was campaigning in the electorate of Coogee. Prime Minister Whitlam was photographed at Coogee Beach with 'bikini girls' and "the former Rugby League Kangaroo winger, Michael Cleary," the Labor candidate for Coogee.[73] In response, Askin campaigned for Ross Freeman. Freeman was a 26-year-old barrister, who was described as resembling a young 'surfie' rather than a politician, and probably needed all the support that could be mustered. So, Askin arrived at the Coogee Bay Hotel on that balmy Friday afternoon prior to the election, flanked by two beautiful 'Go-Go' girls.[74] With a wink and a smile, he made his way across the greasy tiles of the public bar with the girls in tow; the wall-to-wall blue singlet clad male patrons erupted into a cacophony of 'catcalls' and cheers.

Askin was rewarded at the ballot box with a strong majority. Freeman defeated the high-profile Michael Cleary by eight votes. There is no doubt that the boy from Glebe, who rose to the position of premier and the first citizen of the state, always retained the common touch and never forgot his roots.[75]

This brief review of Askin's life and his political record through the five elections in which he led his party reveals a leader possessed of skills that were a principal factor in determining his party's success over the period in which he held office. These skills enabled him comfortably to pass those tests that might be used to predict or assess a government's leader's performance, such as those proposed here: awareness of the needs of peers; maintaining the authority to lead; insight and adaptability to changing political circumstances; and the capacity to meet the requirement to focus on the needs of voters.

Askin's success as a political leader does not raise him above criticism, of course, or excuse him from controversy. Indeed, Askin's reputation has probably suffered more from his involvement or alleged involvement in controversy than has the reputation of any other premier. This might be simply because of the length of time in which he served in this role, or possibly because of the casual way that Askin was prepared to shrug off attacks on his character; but for whatever reason, a few of the incidents and allegations involving the name of Bob Askin deserve mention in any assessment of his record. These few controversies would include: the Sydney Opera House, his "run over the bastards" attitude, the 'green bans' issue, and the allegations of corruption. The last of these merits deeper analysis, because whether they were true or false, they reflect the worst features of Australian politics.

Controversial Issues

The Sydney Opera House

The principal protagonists in the controversy surrounding the Sydney Opera House were the Danish architect Jørn Utzon, the Cahill Labor Government that instigated the project and the Askin Government that completed it. All three deserve their share of criticism. However, it is remarkable that such a masterpiece was conceived, financed and completed. Therefore, all three parties also deserve their rightful accolades.

The Askin Government has sometimes been portrayed as comprising of a bunch of philistines who chased the sensitive genius Utzon out of the country.[76] The responsible minister Davis Hughes in particular, had been accused of being the principal perpetrator. This was dispelled in a letter from Utzon to Philippa Hughes after her husband's death on 16 March 2003. The letter was released by the Hughes family to the *SMH* and printed on 14-15 October 2006. Utzon's letter read as follows:

> Please believe me. I'm very sorry I didn't get to talk to him. Please tell her that I'm very lucky that the building was finished at all. Sydney got that building because of him and his support of Peter Hall and Hall Todd and Littlemore architects. He gave them all the best support. I'm sorry I didn't get time to tell him.
>
> How can a man who has never built anything follow in the same way I was intending? The architecture

wasn't the same but you can't repair Beethoven's symphony by asking Mozart to repair the second half.

I am very sorry I had difficulties in meeting him. He was completely sincere in his dealing with me and what he said about the costs and what kind of a theatre he could build in Armidale for 25 million pounds. My wife is here. She knows what a difficult thing it was to have a husband working on it.

Say to Phillipa she must have my kisses and my comfort for his passing. I'm so grateful the building had his enormous force behind the project and he finished it. It was because of him that the complicated building was finished at all.[77]

US Presidential Visit to NSW: "Run over the Bastards"

October 1966 saw the first visit to Australia of a serving United States President, Lyndon B. Johnson (LBJ). The excitement and enthusiasm which enveloped Sydney in anticipation of a four-hour visit from Texan born President was palpable. The city streets were draped in a mass of red, white and blue bunting, with many buildings displaying pictures of the President. The designated route from Kingsford-Smith Airport for the presidential motorcade was renamed for the day in Johnson's honour.[78] The motorcade was to be showered with ticker-tape at strategic intervals.[79] There were 100,000 free US and Australian flags distributed, while 1,000 school children greeted the President wearing Texan cowboy hats.[80] All children in NSW under the age of 15 were offered free travel to Sydney.[81] The entrance to the formal reception area for the presidential party at the NSW Art Gallery was adorned with a display of caged kangaroos and koalas.[82] A Vietnam Committee which represented all the peace and anti-Vietnam war organisations was formed to organise a mass legal and peaceful "anti-Vietnam war demonstration".[83]

In the midst of all the exuberance Askin demonstrated his artistic flair by suggesting that "beach towels could be hung from the windows to brighten the city". Askin has sometimes been referred to as a philistine, and, after his artistic contribution, this claim might have some merit. Not to be upstaged by Prime Minister Holt's slogan "all the way with LBJ," Askin endorsed the slogan "make Sydney gay for LBJ".[84] The view was expressed that Askin was "overdoing the welcoming".[85]

The motorcade was involved in some dramatic events during the journey from the airport to the Art Gallery. There was a high-speed detour when the posse of US security staff outmanoeuvred an unauthorised anti-Vietnam demonstration which threatened to block the route near the University of New South Wales (UNSW) on Anzac Parade. This caused disappointment for the thousands of well-wishers who had spent hours waiting for the motorcade, only to be rewarded by a flash of glass and chrome as the vehicles sped past.[86] Children wept, whilst some adults cursed that "Sydney has been taken for a ride" and threw their flags into the gutter in disgust.[87]

The vehicles sped too quickly for the ticker-tape to be effective but not quickly enough to escape the accuracy of the flour bombs hurled by the anti-Vietnam war demonstrators "who provided the biggest anti-Vietnam, anti-LBJ demonstration".[88] The air conditioning of the bubble top Cadillac failed after the cooling system was blocked by streamers. Subsequently, the President and his wife, Lady Bird, were rescued by Askin and travelled with the Premier in the fleet of government cars for the remainder of the journey. As the motorcade continued it was halted several times while the police dragged away the demonstrators who had flung themselves in front of the cars.[89] Just as the drama seemed to be subsiding, and with the Art Gallery finally in sight, the President was upstaged by an escaping koala.[90]

In the context of the modern staging of such events, the four-hour sojourn of President Johnson was farcical. However, it was 1966 and Askin had orchestrated an extravaganza with a broad overarching benefit for all involved. Askin had a lively day with LBJ and he commented that "Sydney rose to the occasion. It could never have been better".[91] LBJ enjoyed extensive and favourable US press coverage.[92] The visit was touted as the "biggest reception in Australia's history" and it was declared that "Hollywood couldn't have done it better".[93] The anti-Vietnam war movement received world-wide coverage of their cause;[94] some 'bush kids' were able to visit Sydney for the first time; and one hundred and forty churchmen from Australia and the United States including three bishops from Protestant churches in Australia took advantage of the opportunity to present a signed statement urging the President to deescalate the hostilities in Vietnam. On their way back to the airport, after a harbour cruise, the President endeared himself to some of the disappointed crowd. He stopped the motorcade four times. He threw his ten gallon Texan hat into the delighted crowd at the Sydney Town Hall, exchanged handshakes and 'howdies' before boarding the US Air Force jet bound for the Vietnam war conference in Manila.[95] Ironically, Indigenous Australians were spared from participating in the excruciating event. In contrast to their Maori counterparts, they were excluded from the festivities. At the Wellington airport in New Zealand, *en route* to Australia, the President received a traditional Maori welcome in the form of a war dance performed by Maori tribesman.[96]

Askin demonstrated his insight and adaptability by providing a 'three ring circus' for the voter when he orchestrated the presidential visit. He promoted himself and the government by bathing in the limelight and the popularity of President Johnson. He instilled pride in the voters by showcasing the harbour city to the world. His leadership authority was enhanced when he positioned himself by the side of the most powerful man on earth, particularly in the context of the anxieties of the Cold War, whereby Australia considered the US its great and powerful ally.

Alongside the President, Askin was able to project his

self-image as dependable, beneficent and respectable. His respect and adulation for authority was reflected by his exuberance over the event. This was the occasion when Askin uttered the legendary "run over the bastards" comment in private with the President when referring to the demonstrators. The President was amused by the "back slapping" laconic humour, but the joke would later come back to haunt Askin.

At the airport President Johnson told the press that the demonstrators had the right to dissent.[97] He also embraced Askin with a Texan bear hug and told him; "we have never had a greater welcome than Sydney gave us".[98] According to David McNicoll, a former journalist with *The Bulletin*; there is no doubt that Askin made a great impression on the President. Many years later McNicoll spent a day with Johnson at his ranch in Texas where he "enquired warmly": "How's Bob Askin? ... Now there's a man".[99]

Askin's skill as a consummate raconteur was savoured by the guests who attended the US Chamber of Commerce luncheon in Sydney on 23 July 1968. He was clapped and cheered when he told them that President Johnson was amused when he advised a police officer to "run over the bastards." During Johnson's visit to Sydney on 22 October 1966, Askin was travelling with the President and was referring to the demonstrators who were blocking the motorcade.[100] Askin was never repentant over the alleged incident. On the contrary, in his posterity interview with Mel Pratt he said; "Oh yes, oh well that's not alleged, I said it all right, but it was said jocularly".[101] It was unfortunate for Askin that a reporter overheard the story at the luncheon and it subsequently became the subject of headlines in the tabloid press. Nonetheless, it was politically careless and demonstrated the same lapse into hubris which marred Askin's political judgement at the Georges River by-election.

'Green Bans'

There is no doubt that Askin was on the wrong side of history regarding the 'green bans.' Askin had grown up in Glebe, some of which had deteriorated into a slum and, as with many of his generation, there was a mentality of 'out with the old, in with the new.' Like many people of such backgrounds, Askin did not see many votes at the time in new issues like urban conservation.

The 'green ban' was the result of an alliance between the Builders Labourers' Federation (BLF) and green or environmental conservation groups. They were usually instigated by resident groups or groups advocating environmental protection and conservation. In NSW, the 'green bans' had their genesis when the BLF successfully supported the "Battlers for Kelly's Bush" in their quest to save parkland on the banks of the Parramatta River at Hunter's Hill.[102]

The support of the 'green bans' by the community reflected the sympathetic community attitudes towards the environment and heritage buildings. The bans also served as a bridle against Askin's outdated notion that progress and development were measured "in terms of Sydney's rising skyline".[103] Nevertheless, insufficient voters were engaged in the issue and the controversy created by the 'green bans' had little effect on Askin's electoral success. In other words, as far as Askin was concerned, the 'care factor was zero.' In retrospect, this flawed judgment was uncharacteristic of Askin's demonstrated skill of assessing public sympathy and voting intentions.

The Askin corruption myth

The Askin corruption myth was able to be propagated because the accusations were underpinned by the undisputed fact that organised crime increased during the latter period of the Askin Government, which was manifest by the number of illegal casinos in operation. This was pertinent to the allegations made in the exposé that "Askin and Police Commissioner Hanson were each paid $100,000 per year from 1967-8 until Askin's retirement to allow Perce Galea's illegal casino to operate uninterrupted".[104] However, this conclusion ignores the history of organised crime in NSW in the periods before and after the Askin Government, along with the high likelihood that illegal casinos and organised crime would have escalated under any government during those years.

Without the prosecution of this principal headline

claim, all of the hearsay, innuendo and anonymous accusations are unlikely to have appeared in the public domain. Consequently, it would have been unlikely for the myth to exist, let alone take on a life of its own. As a result, the charge that Askin was "a friend to organised crime" has taken on mythical proportions and become received wisdom.

The Askin corruption myth began with the publication of a profile of Perce Galea in the *National Times* in January 1981. This was followed by the Askin "exposé" on 13 September 1981, and an accusation of corruption made by a group of bookmakers on 27 September 1981. The article concerning the bookmakers was the final publication in the *National Times* by any investigative journalists, in relation to the allegations, that Askin was corrupt. Four years later, David Hickie published a book, *The Prince and the Premier*.

The emergence of the Askin myth and the political environment and circumstances which were conducive for it to be propagated are examined and analysed. A reassessment has been undertaken of the evidence and the commentary over the past 39 years. It has included interviews with some of the protagonists and it is concluded that the Askin corruption myth was founded on hearsay, innuendo and uncorroborated evidence. The Askin myth emerged from the exposé in the *National Times*. As a result of its propagation in *The Prince and the Premier*, the corruption myth became entrenched in the historiography of the period.

Corruption and organised crime

Organised crime has existed in NSW since the colonial era, usually referred to in the past as gang or underground activity. In keeping with the global phenomenon, a new form of sophisticated organised crime syndicate based on the US Mafia model emerged following the gang wars that erupted in Australia in 1967 and 1968.[105] The syndicate leaders were intelligent people who employed the services of accountants, lawyers and highly qualified businessmen to conceal their illegal activities by laundering money through sophisticated offshore facilities, and to defend them or their counterparts when they were prosecuted.[106] The tentacles of these syndicates reached into all aspects of crime such as SP bookmaking, drug trafficking, prostitution and illegal casinos. In the early 1970s, due to the US government's crackdown on the Mafia, their organisations were forced to move their assets to offshore locations, one of which was Australia. The Royal Commission into Organised Crime in Clubs in New South Wales chaired by Justice Moffitt, established by the Askin Government in 1973, discovered that Bally Australia Pty Limited, which was a subsidiary of the Mafia controlled Bally Corporation of America, had attempted to infiltrate Australian clubs.[107]

Between 1973 and 1984, five royal commissions into organised crime were established: the Moffitt, Woodward, Williams, Stewart, and Costigan inquiries.[108] It was revealed that between 1979 and 1984, there was an alarming "escalation in organised crime, both as to amount and sophistication". The upsurge commenced in the mid-1970s, which was after Askin retired.[109]

Athol Moffitt, who was the first royal commissioner to investigate organised crime in Australia, concluded that the adversarial Westminster system allowed for no common ground to be reached concerning issues like organised crime. Instead, the opposing parties were more interested in scoring points by accusing each other of corruption to cause electoral damage. This enabled organised crime, with its intelligence, to enter "unnoticed, from the wings" and exploit the weaknesses in the institutions and politics.[110] Also, apathy and the lack of awareness of most members of the public and many politicians contributed to its escalation.[111] As a result, the hundreds of millions of dollars in profits "[gave] enormous power to the unscrupulous criminals who run large established operations outside the law, in accordance with their own law and in defiance of the nation and its governments, but under the shelter of the freedoms which they provide".[112]

Most evidence persuasively indicates that organised crime would have established itself during the early 1970s no matter which party was in government. The illegal casinos that surfaced during the term of the Askin Government were a result of the global phenomenon of the institutionalisation of organised crime and its subsequent escalation. This is evidenced by the number of illegal casinos under the succeeding governments: there were 13 under the Askin

Government, eleven under the Wran Government, and twenty under the Greiner Government which held office for a much shorter period than either the Askin or Wran governments.

The emergence of the Askin corruption myth

The key to the Askin corruption myth lies buried in the book *Heralds and Angels: The House of Fairfax*, authored by Gavin Souter, who was the Fairfax company's historian.[113] The protagonists responsible for the Askin corruption myth were the inexperienced young journalist David Hickie, the inexperienced editor of the *National Times*, David Marr, and an alleged anonymous primary source whom Hickie described as "impeccable".[114] The primary source was reportedly Perce Galea,[115] "a major crime figure,"[116] who "laundered large amounts of drug money,"[117] and had been dead for four years when the exposé was published.

Percival John Galea was born at Broken Hill on 26 October 1910 and relocated with his family in 1914 to the Sydney suburb of Woolloomooloo.[118] Galea began his career in illegal gambling during World War II when the aristocratic game of baccarat became for many the preferred form of illegal gambling. These "baccarat clubs" took root in the Kings Cross area, which was a popular recreation venue for war servicemen.[119] During the 1970s, Galea and his long-time business partners, Joe Taylor and Eric O'Farrell, and his fellow illegal casino owner, George Walker, transformed these clubs into "fully fledged casinos".[120] Galea became "the uncrowned king of illegal casinos in Sydney".[121]

Galea's associates, and sometime business partners, included the notorious criminals of the day: Lennie McPherson, Abe Saffron, "Stan the Man" Smith and George Freeman.[122] Leonard Arthur 'Lennie' McPherson (1921-1996) "was a standover man, a murderer, a rapist and a thief".[123] Abraham 'Abe' Gilbert Saffron (1919-2006) "was a highly successful Australian criminal whose tentacles of vice, exploitation, gross abuse of the laws of the land, blackmail and corruption … extended across most of mainland Australia and probably overseas for more than half a century".[124] Stanley John 'Stan the Man' Smith (1937-2010) was "one of Sydney's criminal heavyweights for three decades … [and was] described during his prime as a Mafia associate, a 'stand-over criminal and international shop thief".[125] George David Freeman (1935-1990) was a "criminal, gambler and racing commission agent," and a "close confederate of Galea".[126] He was known as the "Boss" in the Sydney crime milieu and was mentioned in several royal commissions into organised crime.[127]

The Askin corruption myth evolved in the following circumstances. At the beginning of 1981, David Marr succeeded Evan Whitton as editor of *The National Times*. Marr was a "young lawyer journalist who had written a widely acclaimed biography of Sir Garfield Barwick".[128] He had demonstrated his ability as a writer and on this basis, Max Suich, the chief editorial executive responsible for the final decision concerning publication, promoted him to editor.[129] Vic Carroll, who was credited with the success of *The Australian Financial Review*, spent only a month mentoring Marr in the art of editorship. Marr was then left to his own devices.[130]

At the time of Marr's promotion, Askin had become seriously ill. David Hickie had been a "close observer and to some extent a confidant of the Galea organisation, which until Perc Galea's death in 1977 had been one of the most important sections of organised crime in Sydney." Hickie was reportedly in possession of "very convincing evidence that the organisation had made regular payments to Askin and many senior police". In anticipation of Askin's death, Marr requested Hickie to broaden his evidence through further investigation.[131]

The publication of the Galea profile in *The National Times* in January 1981 was in anticipation of the Askin exposé, which was to be published the moment Askin was dead. The Galea story begins with the introduction of Professor John Hickie, "one of Sydney's leading... [cardiac] specialists," to Galea in July 1963.[132] After suffering a serious heart attack, Galea had been admitted to St. Vincent's Hospital where he was given a few hours to live. As a prominent Catholic he had received the last rites from Cardinal Norman Gilroy. Galea was a Knight of Saint John, which was the highest papal honour that a Catholic could receive. A nun had informed Hickie that it was "a passport to heaven." (However, there were rumours that Galea had acquired his "passport to heaven" by dubious means). The next morning when Professor Hickie was doing his rounds, he called in to see the new cardiac patient. Galea recovered, and "this was the beginning of a fifteen year friendship".[133]

According to the article, Galea's generosity was well known. "He would arrive at the Professor's house every Christmas night in a truck loaded with [an] enormous 25 foot Christmas [stocking] ... The several hundred dollars' worth of contents were for the Professor's seven children". "Galea loved a night out. He took the Professor to see Nelson Eddy at the old Chequers and Jane Powell at the Chevron, always in the front seat". Professor Hickie noted Galea's generosity and recalled: "I always thought he over tipped the headwaiter". Of course, Galea extended this generosity to his own family: "He was especially careful to look after his family; the ticket that won $200,000 in a lottery in 1975 was called family. We are always in everything together".[134]

Hickie narrates the grand life of Galea at the racecourse. He explains how the £12,000 that Galea won in a lottery in 1957 was seminal to his "meteoric rise as a punter." Galea was "always elegantly, expensively and immaculately attired, and he soon became known as 'The Prince' in racing circles ... He loved to share his success with everyone and was known to be one of the 'softest touches' in the racing game ... more than any other racing identity Galea took the public into his confidence".[135] In March 1964, Galea's horse Eskimo Prince won the Golden Slipper Stakes at Rosehill in Sydney, and Galea won £30,000, whereupon:

> Perc received one of the greatest receptions ever heard of on a Sydney racecourse and in his exuberance Galea pulled out a role of 10 pound notes (totalling 150 pounds) as he was walking up the stairs of the members stand ... and threw it over the fence to the excited crowd. They scrambled in all directions to get the money. Before he left the course he gave away another 1500 pounds to strappers, acquaintances and well-wishers ... Galea always said he owed his incredible luck to a battered old pair [sic] of rosary beads. [136]

Galea was given an air of respectability by references to his operating "upper class casinos in the European style ... Galea invested a small fortune in expensive fixtures in his casinos. But he knew his assets were secure ... For more than ten years the casinos flourished without police interference".[137] Galea probably invested heavily in his casinos in the hope that they would be licenced, because this would have given him the "prominence and respectability" that he so anxiously desired.[138] Licensed casinos had been opened in Tasmania and South Australia and there were rumblings that the NSW government would take similar action.[139] Galea certainly was in a position to capitalise on a change of legislation. His bridge club had an annual turnover of up to $110 million with profits as high as $2.3 million.[140] Given the large amounts involved Galea could easily have paid Askin the amounts claimed by Hickie in his subsequent Askin exposé.

The article laid the ground for the reader to be anchored in the perception that Galea is respectable, prominent, honest and generous. Galea acquired his apparent respectability from his association with Professor Hickie. It was inconsequential that, according to the article, they only socialised on two occasions. Galea's prominence was a result of his racing interests. The implied honesty was based on the notion that, if Galea's "upper class casinos in the European style" were operating in Europe, they would be legal. Galea's generosity was ubiquitously illustrated throughout the article.

In early September 1981, when the news broke that Askin had the dreaded 'death rattle,' and his demise was nigh, the eager "young" journalist and the "elegant" young editor anxiously awaited the publication of their explosive exposé.[141] This could possibly have been the chance of a lifetime for each of them, with a story that might be seen as the Australian equivalent of the American 'Watergate' scoop. Unfortunately, their 'Deep Throat' was "a major crime figure,"[142] who had "laundered large amounts of drug money" and had been dead for four years.[143]

Marr insisted on publishing the article immediately after they received word that Askin was dead. Suich, who had extensive experience and expertise in editorship, and had been a former editor of *The National Times,* was apprehensive due to the lack of documentary evidence. Eventually, he relented because he believed that an editor should possess the necessary skills to judge the veracity and the volume of on-the-record evidence to "justify unsourced assertions".[144]

Hickie was emphatic that the "source is impeccable," adding "this information has not been available for the *National Times* to use until Askin's death".[145] The astonishing fact about this exposé is that Hickie describes Galea without naming him, as "a major crime figure".[146] It is likely that if Galea, who had been dead for four years, had been named as the "impeccable source," Max Suich would not have allowed the exposé to be published and the Askin corruption myth would never have taken hold.

However, the story was published and the premise from which the Askin corruption myth evolved was headlined on the front page: "While Sir Robert Askin was in power, organised crime became institutionalised on a large scale in NSW for the first time. Sydney became the crime capital of Australia".[147] The story is continued on a subsequent page where the reader is informed that: "The casinos produce money for crime, but more importantly they laundered large amounts of drug money".[148] It is implied that Askin was responsible for the escalation of drug trafficking. This underlying process of implication leading to inference dovetailed well with what had been making news at the time. The Woodward Royal Commission into Drug Trafficking (1977-1979) had been initiated to investigate drug trafficking and the disappearance of the anti-drug campaigner Donald Mackay. The Commission had found that the Calabrian Mafia had a powerful influence on drug trafficking in NSW. The subsequent Stewart Royal Commission into Drug Trafficking (1981-83) was set up to investigate the "Mr Asia" drug syndicate.[149] That syndicate had run a multi-national heroin enterprise that had left a litany of murders in its wake.[150] *The Bulletin* published a book review of *Greed,* authored by Richard Hall, which explored the Mr Asia drug syndicate.[151] *The National Times* surveyed allegations "that drugs and other valuable commodities have been smuggled in and out of Australia inside corpses and coffins".[152]

The timing of Hickie's article was derided as outrageous. Lady Mollie Askin was demonstratively upset.[153] Askin's staff, the former ministers who served in the Askin Government, as well as Sir John Carrick and Sir Roden Cutler, all denied "any evidence of systemic corruption". John O'Hara, the *SMH* political correspondent, after scrutinising the rumours and claims, concluded that they were unfounded.[154]

The exposé created a furore. Neville Wran, the Labor Premier, dismissed *The National Times* report as "tasteless in the extreme." Wran said that the [Stewart Royal Commission] ... had the power to inquire into links between Sir Robert Askin and organised crime". Nothing, however, was forthcoming. Wran added that "illegal casinos had always flourished in Sydney ... Australians would bet on two flies crawling up a wall ... some of the most respected people in society frequented the casinos ... from his point of view it would be better if the casinos were legalised".[155] Wran, who had been premier since 1976, found himself in the same position as Askin regarding the eradication of organised crime and concurred with Moffitt that politicisation, apathy and lack of public awareness made the issue almost intractable.

John Singleton, an advertising man and media commentator described Hickie as "that little cowardly person who wrote that attack on Bob Askin yesterday, free of any facts, just smears and innuendos of a petty mind, and to think that the once great Fairfax empire could stoop to such gutter, gutless journalism is to me sickening".[156] *The Daily Telegraph* reported "a storm of anger".[157] *The Daily Mirror* headlined the report as "Despicable" and noted that the allegations were concerned with dead people.[158]

The National Times made the following statement in reply to these criticisms: "In response to our story last week a great deal of fresh information has been added to *The National Times* material on corruption in the Askin and later years". This was confirmed by Marr in a television appearance. The decision to publish the day before Askin's funeral was viewed "as the most wilful infringement of the maxim against speaking evil of the dead".[159] Suich had overlooked the usual procedure of consulting James Fairfax, the Chairman of the Board of John Fairfax and Sons, when contentious issues were to be published. Subsequently, Suich was left with the unenviable task to show cause to the board why he and Marr should not resign.[160]

The concern of Sir Warwick Fairfax, a Board member and former chairman, was that the publication of such an article "brought discredit to the whole organisation." The directors were concerned that the allegations were made the moment Askin was dead, and not during the past 16 years since he had become premier. The Board issued a memo to Suich to be passed on to Marr and the deputy editor, Brian Toohey.[161] There is no doubt that the Board members remembered that Askin had a defamation writ issued against Fairfax over an article in the "Clancy" section of *The National Times* on 21 September 1980. The Board accepted responsibility for the libel, and the apology was subsequently published in *The National Times*.[162] There was ample opportunity for any evidence to be tested. Fairfax was in a position to "call their witnesses under oath, cross examine Askin ruthlessly, examine all his financial affairs, expose his bank accounts, [because] once a writ is issued, the matter must proceed to its final conclusion in court, except with the agreement … of all parties".[163] John Fairfax & Sons made the decision not to proceed.

The memo read:

> No further story relating to Sir Robert Askin is to be published unless you have persuasive and hard on-the-record evidence. This is not to say that you can't use anonymous sources where you are satisfied of their honesty and accuracy, but the reputation of The National Times must not be prejudiced by serious charges being made by simple assertions.[164]

In other words, the Board considered Hickie's evidence was nothing more than "simple assertions". Under a more experienced editor like Suich, the article would probably not have been published.

Suich initially agreed to Marr's request to publish a follow-up article. However, after Marr appeared on a television show and promised to publish it, Suich changed his mind. Perhaps Suich objected to being pressured by Marr and the television station. After some heated debate, "Suich said reluctantly: [to Marr] ok it's on your head".[165]

The second and final article was written by Hickie and Marian Wilkinson and published in the 27 September-3 October 1981 issue of *The National Times*.[166] The article "asserted that Sir Robert, in the last few months of his premiership, had been paid $55,000 by a group of Sydney bookmakers to ensure that bookmakers' turnover tax was not increased".[167] A rumour had been circulating that the licenced bookmakers' turnover tax was to be doubled. The authors were indifferent to the fact that after Askin retired, Premier Lewis doubled the tax. The second article made no significant corruption claims and Suich appeared satisfied, probably because he was not compelled to bear the wrath of James Fairfax and the Board.[168] In actuality, the article was about a typical bunch of greedy bookmakers carping about money. Askin had announced his retirement and decisions were in the hands of his successors.[169] So after clear instructions from the Fairfax Board to produce "persuasive and hard on-the-record evidence," [170] this was all that was forthcoming.

The propagation of the Askin corruption myth

The Prince and the Premier was published on Thursday 28 March 1985. It was launched with a flurry of publicity. The book expanded on the theme introduced in the exposé, specifically that Askin was responsible for the institutionalisation of organised crime and was thus culpable for the major criminal activities making headlines in all the major newspapers of the day. Galea's respectability was enhanced and the "impeccable source" remained a mystery.

Marr who had enthusiastically endorsed the exposé when he was editor of *The National Times* appears to have lost faith in Hickie's evidence when he concluded that the book was "extraordinarily repetitive" and had only an "odd ring of truth". After four years of reflection, Marr's assessment is significant in so far as it brings Hickie's evidence into contention.[171] Marr was more measured in his portrayal of Galea and Askin;

this is in contrast to Hickie's "impeccable source" and the characterisation of Galea as the hero and Askin as the villain.[172] If Marr was fully convinced of Hickie's evidence, it is unlikely that he would have equivocated with such a weak turn of phrase as "odd ring of truth". Instead, Marr left the interpretation wide open to the reader and omits to present Hickie's evidence and assessment as an accurate and truthful account of Askin.

According to Marr, Hickie's account rested on a view that: "The scale of the operation and the network of criminal activity which flourished under Askin's active patronage were known at the time". However, he dismissed Hickie's view when he concluded that "Askin was only an inheritor, taking up and perfecting what had been developed by his predecessors who had come to office promising reform and retired leaving the system functioning".[173] Marr opined that Askin got "away with it" because the press "with a few honourable exceptions" were corrupted by men like Galea.[174]

Meanwhile, probate had been granted for the Askin estate and the headlines in the *Sun Herald* 31 March 1985 read "Tax man hits Askin Will".[175] This might have passed unnoticed if the book had not been published at the same time. Also on 27 March 1985, the day before the book was published, Max Newton, an expatriate and journalist living in New York, and founding editor of *The Australian,* made the sensational claim on a Sydney radio program that, prior to entering parliament, Neville Wran had facilitated a bribe from Filipino businessman Felipe Ysmel to Askin.[176] After the fracas that the allegations caused, Newton said "I underestimated how amenable the climate was to talk of political corruption these days".[177] The fracas certainly would not have stalled the sale of Hickie's book.

Newton claimed that in 1971 he had been asked by Wran, then a Queen's Counsel (QC), to deliver $15,000 to Askin on behalf of his client, Ysmel "a [Filipino] multi-millionaire steel magnate who was one of the biggest punters in Australia"[178] and who was seeking to persuade Askin to approve plans that would allow him to build a sports stadium for Jai Lai, "a game associated with high betting".[179] Newton had made an enquiry as to whether Askin would receive a donation for the 1971 election campaign and concluded that Askin was happy to take the donation, and in return Ysmel hoped to gain an interview.[180] With regard to the money, Newton said "I've never seen $15,000 disappear so quick [into the top draw]. I'm afraid Bob [Askin] didn't deliver".[181] If there is any truth in the claim, then Ysmel, in his attempt to bribe Askin, suffered the same fate as the bookmakers.

Wran immediately provided the NSW Police Commissioner with a statutory declaration denying the allegation and tabled it in Parliament.[182] In describing Newton, Wran said:

> Newton owes the Commonwealth Taxation Commissioner hundreds of thousands of dollars, he is a tax cheat, a tax avoider and a bankrupt ... Since dead men tell no tales and in the atmosphere of guilt by association which permeates the fabric of Australian society today, Newton, this whisky swilling eccentric, with a reputation for unreliability and instability has decided to seek a headline for himself ... Anyone who believes Newton's allegation, would be prepared to believe that the Pope is a Jew.[183]

The *Sunday Telegraph* took it upon itself to investigate the allegations and concluded that "it was nothing but a storm in a teacup". Newton's affidavit was published in the *Sunday Telegraph* outlining the incident and the paper was satisfied that "Newton does not even hint at any criminal activity".[184] After Police Commissioner John Avery investigated the allegations, he concluded in his report that "All of these issues, when coupled with the fact that this meticulous investigation has elicited not one item of corroboration, convinces me, as I have said, that the claims Maxwell Newton are utterly without foundation".[185] Wran was sympathetic to the injustice of an atmosphere that led to the implication that Askin was guilty by association but, whereas this spurred Wran on to defend himself vigorously, Askin could not do the same because he was dead.

In the same week that the Hickie book was published *The Sun Herald* published an article about Lady Mollie Askin who had died in 1984. The paper claimed that her $3,724,879 estate, including Askin's estate, had been substantially reduced. This was because "investigators checked bookmakers' ledgers and other sources" which prompted "a taxation inquiry into Sir Robert's affairs".[186] The tax debt was reported to be $2 million, but despite the serious implication of this assertion, the source of the information was not identified. The *Sun-Herald* newspaper pointed out that: "An official of the Permanent Trustee Company LTD., the administrators of the Askin estate, said ... the amount of tax is confidential – a matter between the client and the taxation department. The estate had been reduced by taxation and other creditors ... There was still a substantial residue and the legacies would be paid in full. And there will be quite a handsome amount to go to charities".[187] It is worth mentioning that long after the fanfare surrounding the publication of the Hickie book had subsided, the headlines read: "Hospitals get most of Askin's cash". The trustees relayed that the "tax settlement was not as big as suggested in earlier reports ... When [Lady Askin] died in 1984 she left gifts of $1.4 million to friends and charities and directed the remaining $2.5 million be invested in two perpetual funds to benefit charities and welfare groups".[188]

Reassessment of the Askin corruption allegations

Bob Bottom is one of the more important and respected figures in investigating and reporting on organised crime in Australia. He sparked his first inquiry into the NSW Police Force with an exposé in *The Bulletin* magazine in 1963. He was credited with expediting Australia's first royal commission into organised crime – the Moffitt Royal Commission in NSW in 1973. Since that time, he has participated in 18 royal commissions and other judicial and parliamentary inquiries. In 1997 he was awarded an Order of Australia Medal (OAM) in recognition of his work.

The principal allegation that Askin was paid $100,000 per year from 1967-8 until his retirement, to allow Galea's illegal casinos to operate with impunity, defies logic. According to Bottom, "there has never been any first-hand proof that [Askin] personally received any bribe money relating to illegal casinos". Bottom continued: "No police intelligence reports or telephone intercept records which I had access to ever detected anything linked to Askin" and doubted if "Askin really did receive any bribe money to allow" casinos to continue to operate. He also noted that "illegal casinos continued to flourish" under all succeeding governments and yet, "unlike the legendary singling out of Askin, nobody has ever suggested, in the media or in parliament, that Lewis, Wran, Unsworth or Greiner received any bribe money for allowing virtually the same number of illegal casinos to flourish for two decades after Askin retired."[189]

This was further substantiated in the 1987 NSW Police Commissioner's Organised Crime Group report which found that "Total eradication of gambling was not the intent of the legislative change, as it was realised that as with Prohibition in the [US], such an objective was doomed to failure. There does exist today, however, various forms of illegal gambling in this state".[190] The inquiry by the former Chief Justice of NSW Supreme Court, Sir Laurence Street, into a proposed bill to legalise casinos in 1991 discovered that there were twenty illegal casinos operating in Sydney and "numerous small ethnic gambling clubs".[191] "The introduction of legal casinos in Sydney is unlikely to eliminate illegal casino gambling," Sir Laurence concluded "although it may diminish to some extent ... It was unrealistic to expect that such activity could be eliminated entirely".[192] This was tabled in State Parliament on 3 December 1991. The New South Wales Independent Commission Against Corruption (ICAC) was told that, "Bruce Galea, son of the late Sydney racing identity Perce Galea, was believed to be the biggest illegal gaming operator in the state".[193] In relation to the last clause in Bottom's statement, allegations were never made that Bruce Galea paid extortion money to any Premier, to enable him to operate with impunity.

Hickie's evidence

With the passage of time, Hickie was prepared to grant the author an interview where he declared that all principal sources could be discussed openly because they were all deceased. Hickie confirmed that almost all of his "24 filing cabinets" of material on Askin had now been discarded, and, as a result, there were no contemporaneous notes forthcoming. Based on a re-examination of the evidence, in conjunction with a lengthy interview with Hickie, the only clear conclusion is that the corruption claim is based on hearsay, innuendo and anonymous accusations.

Galea, who was Hickie's primary source, has already been discounted because he was "a major crime figure," who had "laundered large amounts of drug money" and had been dead for four years.[194] Bob Bottom has also added that it is not credible that Galea would have shared any of the details of his illegal business operations with Hickie, who at the time was a young law student and gardener.[195] The other well-placed sources noted in Hickie's material were Galea's wife Beryl, his long-time business partner Eric O'Farrell and fellow illegal casino boss George Walker.

Regarding Beryl, Bottom notes that "of course they [major criminals] are not telling their wives much about their business operations and in any event, because graft payments were made by go-betweens and well out of the sight of wives, they might know that their husbands are paying people money but they would not know who to".[196] Bottom also notes that major criminals such as O'Farrell and Walker always observed their criminal code and did not disclose confidential matters such as these to anyone, let alone a student and gardener. [Hickie had a lawn-mowing business when he was at university and often spoke to his sources after he had finished mowing their lawn]. This point holds particular weight when considering that Bottom had access to police wire taps of major crime figures such as George Freeman, Abe Saffron and the "boss of bosses" Fred Anderson "who controlled most things".[197] While these tapes do talk about police and 'who ran what', they never refer to the involvement of Askin or politicians. In summary, the claim that Askin was the patron of organised crime in Sydney, presented by Hickie in the book and to the author after 39 years, cannot be sustained.

There appears to be no doubt that Askin engaged the services of SP bookmakers, and, as Jim Carlton (the Liberal Party's General Secretary who succeeded John Carrick) said, Askin had "turned a blind eye" to SP bookmaking, but this could hardly be considered to be systemic corruption.[198] Further, John O'Hara pointed out, Askin was in a position to take advantage of his connections with the 'big end of town' which might have given him an advantage and opportunities in the purchase of shares and property, but O'Hara investigated the rumours concerning the corruption allegations and nothing was forthcoming. David McNicoll was one of only a few journalists who knew Askin personally and this is what he had to say about the allegations:

> If Askin was accepting bribes he had strange ways of enjoying the fruits. His lifestyle was almost depressingly simple. He never aspired to a more glamorous home than a Manly cottage; he entertained hardly at all.[199]

The corruption claim was also anchored in a belief that the size of Askin's estate was too large to have been accumulated via legitimate means. However, the claim by Hickie that the Askin estate could not have been accumulated, based on Askin's income, is naïve and myopic. As noted by Waller, the period of Askin's political career was "times of plenty".[200] For example, the median house price in Sydney rose by almost 700 per cent from $11,800 in June 1965 to $78,740 December 1980;[201] during the same period, the average Australian share price increased by over 400 per cent.[202] Waller also notes that "payment of income tax had become voluntary. There was no capital gains tax, no fringe benefits tax" and in summary "only mugs and public servants" (himself included) paid tax … lump sum of money could be multiplied many times over in a short space of time".[203] One of Askin's Cabinet colleagues has noted privately that Askin had "the deepest pockets he had ever seen" and always managed to save rather than spend every penny he ever made. His idea of an appropriate gift for each of his ministers when he returned from an official visit to North America was a little glass bubble with artificial snow falling on Mexico City.[204] Waller also points out that an intelligent, frugal, well-informed and well-connected man such as Askin could certainly have accumulated his estate without recourse to "dishonourable conduct".[205] A definitive conclusion cannot be made until such time as additional 'concrete evidence' comes to light, such as the release of probate details in 2071.

Even taking Hickie's claims at face value, it would not satisfy the scrutiny of a reasonable person. For example, the evidence of Askin's tax affairs should be discounted as they are unverifiable and based on undocumented information from an unnamed tax office official whom Hickie said could face criminal charges if he identified himself. Regarding knighthoods, there is no compelling evidence that Askin sold knighthoods. For instance, regarding Hickie's allegation that Sir Elton Griffin paid Askin for a knighthood, Hickie's source was an "unnamed former senior bank officer" who claimed Griffin wrote a cheque to Askin for $20,000, but could not provide any evidence that the cheque was payment for his knighthood. The worst that can be said of Askin in this regard is that he might have approved of a knighthood knowing that, along with other qualifications, the nominee had made a legal donation to a political candidate or party.

Galea: the primary "impeccable" source

It has never been suggested that Hickie, "an honest soldier of the truth," ever doubted Galea's word or harboured "the remotest doubt that Askin was corrupt". On the contrary, it is well within the realms of possibility that the inexperienced young journalist was duped by a master of crime. It is important to remember that Galea was Hickie's primary source and that, in view of the need for Galea to cover himself against the possibility of libel charges, the story of possibility that the inexperienced young journalist was duped by a master of crime. It is important to remember that Galea was Hickie's primary source and that, in view of the need for Galea to cover himself against the possibility of libel charges, the story could not be published until Askin was dead. The impressionable Hickie, who was a student at the time and looking to a career in journalism, would have been keen for a story and in the right frame of mind to fall for a Galea fabrication.

The rationale behind Galea's duplicity was probably to mete out retribution upon Askin. Respectability and legitimacy are often desired goals for organised crime figures.[208] In Galea's case this was exemplified by his desire for "entrée into the most privileged circles" and his life-long ambition to become a member of the Sydney Turf Club (STC) and the Australian Jockey Club (AJC).[209] "The race clubs traditionally refused membership to people with … unsavoury reputations … [Galea] had been black-balled for over 20 years".[210] Askin was said to have "extorted" a sum of $5000 from Galea to assist him in his membership to the STC.[211] Galea, however, had been a strong sponsor of the Labor Party and they helped him to obtain a provisional membership of the AJC. Galea said "I feel fulfilled now … After 20 years, I really wanted the badge".[212]

Respectability was probably only one of the reasons why the legalisation of the casinos was of paramount importance to Galea.[213] His illegal gambling enterprises were a financial risk in that they could be closed at any moment.[214] Galea had invested heavily and his capital was always at risk. The capital value of an enterprise earning $2.3 million and with annual turnover of $100 million would have had an enormous value when it was legalised. This might have been utilised as collateral to support legal investments. The legal casinos would reduce the risk of being investigated for tax evasion in relation to other illegal income.[215] Money from illegal activities is easily mixed in with funds from a legitimate business.[216] The lucrative profits gained from the legal casinos could be prudently reinvested in the expansion of these businesses and legitimate employment would have been available to family members and other members of the organised crime fraternity.[217] Galea considered himself a family man, and legalisation of the casinos would have enabled him to bequeath the enterprises and their income to his beneficiaries.[218] He had experienced a series of heart attacks so his legacy is likely to have increasingly played on his mind. If the enterprises had been legitimate, his son Bruce Galea might not have been identified by ICAC as "the biggest illegal gaming operator in the state".[219]

In 1973-74 Galea had reason to be optimistic regarding the legalisation of his casinos. The NSW Government was monitoring the impact of the licenced casino in Tasmania.[220] Also "the annual convention of the state Liberal Party passed a motion urging the NSW Government to legalise gambling clubs immediately".

John Maddison, the Minister for Justice, said he was "in favour of legalising clubs provided existing illegal clubs were brought under control".[221] In August 1974 there was a rumour that Askin was about to nominate two operators to be granted casino licences.[222]

Expectations of the legalisation of the casinos were dashed when Askin stated in Parliament on 27 August 1974, four months before he retired, "I am against the legalising of gambling casinos and there is no question of their being made legal while I am Premier and Treasurer".[223] There is no doubt that this caused disappointment amongst Galea and the organised crime network. This was demonstrated by the vitriol in a tirade by Stanley John Smith, one of Sydney's criminal heavyweights for over three decades, delivered (and recorded) during a meeting of major crime figures at the Taiping Restaurant in Elizabeth Street, Sydney.[224]

The meeting was held on 22 June 1976 just after Premier Wran announced that his government intended to legalise the casinos. Smith had devised a plan whereby the members of the organised crime network would retain control of the casinos when they were licenced. This became known as the Taiping conspiracy. Smith was "revered among criminals as 'Stan the man' [and identified] as a leader of the underworld". His aim was to "get the game sewn up", so that the licences would not be granted to outsiders. This was to be achieved by bribing politicians "to gain control of any board set up to grant licences and administer casinos".[225] Smith claimed "we done the same six years ago, the exact same thing you are facing now".²²⁶ According to Bottom, "It was not clear whether he was suggesting that organised crime in Australia had had a part in Las Vegas or whether he was alluding to the NSW licenced club industry".²²⁷ Smith reminded his confederates of the benefits of having the casinos licenced: "You're talking about something that could go on forever ... [the] government is getting their tax out of it ... This is a legal way of printing money ... you're dealing with a multimillion dollar business there".²²⁸

As the self-appointed overseer of the conspiracy, Smith castigated his confederates for their ineptitude in squandering the opportunity when Askin was premier:

> I've never found you the most generous people that I've fucking heard of. You know, so, perhaps you might be looking at long pennies. For Christ sake, get up and realise you're dealing with a multi-million dollar business there. So, if you sit back and hang back with your traditional penny pinching fucking attitude, well, this'll slip away from you. That is why I started in this whole business, [as overseer] when you didn't do it with fucking Askin. [Sir Robert Askin, former Premier] ... You know, as well as I do, [politicians] they're the shiftiest bunch of fucking people that ever, ever lived.²²⁹

Smith was infuriated with Galea and his cohorts because they were unable to bribe Askin and have their casinos legalised and he did not want to miss another opportunity. Nonetheless, the Wran Government changed its policy and it was almost two decades before a legal casino operated in NSW.

The Moffitt Royal Commission

The establishment of the Moffitt Royal Commission in 1973 concerning the infiltration of organised crime into NSW registered clubs was a result of an exposé, published, by Bob Bottom in the *Sunday Telegraph* 25 July 1972 under the header, "Crims Grab Clubs." It was followed by another 'seminal piece' co-authored by Bottom and Anthony Reeves, "The Night the Mafia Came to Sydney".[230] Until these exposes were published organised crime had largely escaped public attention. Consequently, the Askin Government requested a report from the Police Commissioner regarding the matter. An interim report was prepared which indicated that there was infiltration of organised crime into registered clubs and a serious threat from overseas.[231]

Askin alerted the Parliament to the findings of the interim police report. However, when the final report was handed to the Askin Government, he did not table it in the Parliament as he had promised. The final report was a complete contradiction of the interim report. The South Sydney Juniors' Leagues Club, which had attracted the greatest suspicion in the interim report, was now regarded as completely free of corruption and the "Bally organisation was clean and beautiful".[232] The diligent Opposition under the leadership of Pat Hills declared it a "whitewash" and a "cover up."

In an unprecedented response, Askin established a royal commission and declared that he would take the witness stand. He said, "It was more efficient to give the Police reports to a Royal Commission than to table them in parliament".[233] Justice Randolph Athol Moffitt was appointed commissioner. This was the first royal commission to deal specifically with organised crime: "Maddison said that Askin set up the Royal Commission because of the charges that the (Askin) Government was covering up, and illegalities in the clubs".[234]

The Moffitt Royal Commission certainly shone the spotlight on the 'celebrities' of the organised crime fraternity. If Askin had been involved with organised crime then surely he would have been reluctant to initiate a royal commission. The header in the *Daily Telegraph*, 23 March 1974 read: "Stars appear at club inquiry ... With 'Fibber', 'Blue eyes' and the gang ... It all sounds like a roll call for a hoods' convention." The "American gangsters some of them top Mafiosi" were mentioned because of their connection with 'Bally Manufacturing Corporation of America'... a huge US poker machine company". It was stated by the *Daily Telegraph* to be of great concern that a US crime syndicate had attempted to infiltrate Australia via 'Bally Australia Pty. Ltd'.[235]

The Australian celebrities who made personal appearances by way of subpoena were Abraham Gilbert Saffron, George David Freeman and McPherson, who took centre stage. McPherson was alleged to have pressured licenced clubs to use Bally poker machines. He had taken Joseph Dan Testa to Bourke, NSW on a kangaroo shooting trip. Testa had "become synonymous with accusations of American Mafia infiltration into Australia".[236] He was described by a Commission witness as a psychopathic killer. When he arrived in Australia to give evidence he vowed "revenge against any witness who had named him".[237] In the light of the public airing and the ordeal that Askin inflicted upon these criminals with his decision to appoint a royal commission; the allegation that he was a friend to organised crime makes no sense at all.

The Moffitt Royal Commission began on 3 September 1973, and after an eighty-four day hearing from 154 witnesses, who were asked more than fifty thousand questions, tabled its report in Parliament on 14 August 1974.[238] The Askin Government was exonerated from any charges relating to a 'cover up'. However, Moffitt recommended that the Bally Corporation should be banned from operating in Australia because it posed a threat of infiltration into Australian licenced clubs.[239] Following the release of the Moffitt Report, the Liberal deputy leader Eric Willis told the Parliament that despite question time allegations from current and previous Opposition leaders, none of them agreed to be cross examined or presented a shred of evidence to the Moffitt Royal Commission. The Opposition allegations "dissolved into thin air" and did not resurface in parliament after the release of the commission report despite "the coward's cloak of parliamentary privilege" afforded to the opposition.[240]

Askin told the Parliament, three months later on 4 December 1974, that Hewett and two other cabinet ministers as well as himself had written to the Royal Commission advising that they were "quite willing to go along voluntarily and I was quite happy to give them all the information I had". Askin then complained that members of the Opposition abused their parliamentary privilege to make serious allegations without a shred of evidence had no place in the parliament.[241]

The Waller Report and other protagonists

Justice Athol Moffitt stood by his assessment 20 years later in a letter to Kevin Waller stating that: "There was no evidence, hearsay or otherwise, before the Royal Commission (on Organised Crime in Clubs) over which I presided in 1973 of improper conduct on the part of Sir Robert Askin".[242] In 1993, the *Sun Herald* "took the extraordinary step" of holding a 'commission of inquiry,' overseen by journalist Evan Whitton and led by former NSW Coroner, Kevin Waller, to review the evidence against Askin.[243] This took place after the publication of the Fairfax history *Herald and Angels*, because the Fairfax organisation was probably haunted by the propagation of the Askin corruption myth that had been founded on 'unsourced assertions'. Waller stated in his report

> The main purpose of the procedure is not to convict or acquit an individual, but to search for the truth. However, before public figures may be stigmatised as corrupt one must insist on evidence of some strength.
>
> Where has the evidence come from? I have read David

> Hickie's book "*The Prince and the Premier*," together with his later comment and the further material received at the *Sun-Herald*. Much of the information is remote hearsay, and in many instances the witnesses are dead, unknown, un-named or otherwise unavailable.
>
> No significance at all can be attached to statements by un-named persons. There is not a responsible tribunal in the world which would place any reliance whatever on reported conversations with anonymous people. *The Prince and the Premier* is littered with such quotations, which may have satisfied the author but do not constitute proper evidence for obvious reasons. [244]

Evan Whitton was understandably not interested in the topic after the inquiry by the *Sun Herald* in 1993 turned into a debacle when a lengthy reproach was received from the former Justice Moffitt. Whitton had inaccurately claimed that Askin had committed perjury by swearing under oath that he had never been inside an illegal casino. This was typical of the inaccuracies that fuelled the hearsay and innuendo that were responsible for the myth to take on a life of its own. In fact, Askin made this statement in an interview published in *The Australian*.[245]

At the time of the Waller Report, Stuart Littlemore QC who was commentator for the ABC *Media Watch* program, publicly goaded Hickie to be cross-examined on his evidence. He noted that there were "very embarrassing reasons, aren't there, Mr Hickie, that explain your unwillingness to debate the quality of your work." Littlemore reinforced Waller's observations that

Hickie's evidence was no more than "rumour, tittle-tattle and second and third-hand material" that "will not do" and then told Hickie to "put up or shut up". He also noted that Waller's assessment was contrary to what Whitton had expected.[246] Significantly, two of Waller's most damning pages of the report were omitted from publication.

Wal Fife, Milton Morris, and Sir John Fuller, who were members of Askin's Cabinet throughout the entire period of his premiership, and who enjoyed honourable reputations, were all interviewed and they were all emphatic that Askin was not corrupt.[247] John Hatton, the 'maverick' former independent state parliamentarian for South Coast, who was misreported in the media as having accused Askin of being corrupt confirmed that he was not privy to any evidence that proved Askin was corrupt. His misreported claim was simply that organised crime flourished in the latter part of the term of the Askin Government.[248] It is noteworthy that Hickie used Hatton's misreported statement to support his allegations. Askin's press secretary, Geoff Reading, and Russ Ferguson, who was Askin's driver for over 20 years, and would have been privy to any illegalities were equally emphatic. Reading said that Hickie's claims were "never tested" and remained "unproven." Ferguson said, "if there was anything like that I think I'd know".[249]

John O'Hara, an esteemed journalist of the Askin era, died on June 11, 2018 aged 91. In 1962, O'Hara had moved to the *Herald*'s State Political Bureau and entered his golden age reporting on the era of Premier Robert Askin. In the years that followed, his reporting ranged over the entire spectrum – education, transport, health, finance, Commonwealth-State relations, the Opera House, environment, organised crime, nude beaches, drought, extended hotel trading hours, The Rocks, Botany Bay, Sydney's second airport. In the words of journalist Geoffrey Reading, O'Hara was "the doyen of the NSW Parliamentary press gallery … Askin died in September 1981 and suggestions of corruption were made by the *National Times*, underlined more emphatically by author David Hickie. O'Hara said there was no cogent evidence that Askin was corrupt at all and, though not uncritical of Askin during his years of coverage of state affairs, wrote in defence of him".[250]

Conclusions

Sir Robert Askin was a political leader of rare skill. A year after serving in the AIF during World War II he joined the Liberal Party and three years later in 1950 he was elected to NSW Legislative Assembly as Member for Collaroy. Askin became deputy leader of the Parliamentary Liberal Party in August 1954 and was elected Leader in 1959. He led his party back from the wilderness to victory in 1965 and remained unchallenged as Premier and Treasurer for a decade. Askin retired on 3 January 1975. In retirement, the Askins lived a quiet life. Askin had suffered two heart attacks during his time as premier and his health was not good. He and his wife Molly enjoyed the surrounds of Fairy Bower in Manly; they went to the races, played cards and kept a low profile. They attended the odd official function, usually a farewell to one of his colleagues. He also fulfilled his duties as Director on the board of TNT, a role that added fuel to the rumour that Abeles had paid him for his knighthood which is part of the corruption myth. Askin continued to suffer poor health in the last couple of years of his life and died in September 1981, aged 74.

Upon his death, the *Manly Daily* paid this tribute: "As a politician, he never forgot his roots as a common man. He brought the Liberal Party back to the people, and the people of Pittwater remember in particular his warmth and sincerity as their member for many years".[251]

Throughout his political life, Askin withstood numerous attacks from media that had to be judged as hostile and from opponents, some of whom considered him a class traitor, and even from many on his own side of politics. All this is normal and Askin had an extraordinary capacity to shrug it off. What was not normal and was in fact quite reprehensible was the depth and bitterness of the attacks his reputation was subjected to after he died.

If we were to attribute truth to these attacks, we would have in Askin an unscrupulous politician who was a "friend to organised crime": A man who extorted enormous bribes from major organised crime figures throughout most of his premiership and who was responsible for the escalation and entrenchment of organised crime in NSW.

The allegation that $1,255,000 of the Askin estate went to relatives and friends and "half the remainder of the estate went to establish a perpetual fund for the welfare of animals", along with other claims, was farcical conjecture.[252]

In 2013, Australia's oldest trustee company, Perpetual Trustees, were compelled by the *Australian Charities and Not-for-profits Commission (ACNC) Act 2012* (Cth) to release information regarding Askin charitable trusts. On behalf of Molly Askin and her late husband Sir Robert Askin, four charitable trusts were established in 1982 to be managed in perpetuity by Perpetual Trustees. The largest of those trusts, the hospital trust, has contributed millions to the public hospital system in NSW including almost $1million to Sydney Eye Hospital. The total of the balance sheets of the four trusts currently stands at almost $12 million including $9.3 million in the hospitals trust, $900,000 in the Animal Welfare trust and $750,000 in each of the Ballet Scholarship and Operatic Scholarship trusts.[253]

The allegation against Askin does not pass the scrutiny of time and history. It defies logic and fails the 'pub test'. Askin had no children to benefit from his wealth and he desired no ostentatious status symbols such as mansions, cars, or holiday homes. Askin would not have placed his premiership in jeopardy by engaging in corrupt activities with the intention of bequeathing the vast majority to the citizens of NSW.

Askin's leadership was essential to the Coalition becoming a long-term government and not just a one-term novelty in a Labor state. Before Askin led the Liberals to victory in 1965, they had languished in opposition for 24 years and it appeared that they were doomed to become a 'permanent opposition' party.[254] Despite rare detours into hubris, his leadership underpinned four electoral terms and as such Askin holds the record as the longest serving NSW Liberal Premier.[255]

Regarding the corruption myth, the conclusion reached after interviewing David Hickie, and after reassessing the central allegations that propagated the myth, is that the evidence is based on unsubstantiated and uncorroborated claims. The allegations as stated simply cannot be sustained.

Despite Askin's unmatched record, the corruption myth unfairly tarnished his reputation and consequently there is not one public monument in his name; it is like he never existed. However, 'true to form' he created his own legacy in the form of four charitable trusts of which the bulk went to a Hospital Trust supporting the NSW public hospital system. Today the balance sheets of the four trusts stand at almost $12 million.[256]

Epilogue

On 29 May 2012, during one of my regular visits to the research desk at the NSW State Library I had a chance encounter with David Marr. Upon introducing myself as the person who had contacted him via email regarding the PhD project on the Askin Government, Marr became very agitated. He said, "you people, if I gave an interview to every PhD student on request, I wouldn't have time to do my own work. It's a big project. You can't do that."

His histrionics escalated when he then stated, "I can't help you because I wasn't there." My immediate response was "but you were" to which he retorted, "but only a year". He started kicking the carpet, turning circles, and saying in a sotto voce voice, "fuck, fuck, fuck". He reluctantly agreed to a half hour phone interview. Later I offered him a fee (he indicated his time was valuable) on the assumption he would donate it to one of his favourite charities. The interview was refused on the grounds that the fee offer was "out of line,"[257] but it was clear that Marr had no intentions of being interviewed.

Marr's behaviour became even more 'bizarre' when I returned to my library desk on that fateful day. I looked up and there was this elongated figure leering and lurking and staring menacingly at me as he slowly made his way around the perimeter of the reading room before he left. I must confess I did laugh to myself, it was puerile, but very funny.

But that 'ain't it', the tangled web of the Askin corruption myth just keeps on giving. On the 18 May 2017, journalist Mark Dapin contacted me by email. He was writing a book review for *The Australian* newspaper on the recently published book *Sydney Noir: The Golden Years* authored by Michael Duffy and Nick Hordern. There is a chapter in the book on the Askin corruption myth. The primary source was the author's PhD thesis. It is worth nothing that an interview with Marr for the book was not forthcoming. Dapin stated that he had spoken to David Marr and Marr responded, "Askin was an absolute crook. Publishing Hickie's story within a few hours of Askins (sic) death is one of the best things I've ever done in journalism".

My response to Dapin was, "Where has he [Marr] written or spoken about this great achievement since 1981. Why was he so disparaging, rude, and obnoxious to an ordinary PhD student, if he had nothing to hide. In other words, there was no evidence for the unsubstantiated, uncorroborated allegations made in his career making article, and none presented since." I offered Marr the opportunity to enhance the collective knowledge by way of an interview, but again, he squibbed on the offer. It appears that whenever Marr is challenged regarding the unsubstantiated, uncorroborated allegations he runs for cover up the nearest hollow log.

1Notes

1. Ian Hancock, "Askin, Robin (later Sir Robert)," in David Clune and Ken Turner, (eds), *The Premiers of New South Wales 1856-2005, Volume 2, 1901-2005*, Parliament of NSW and University of Sydney, Sydney, 2006, p. 364; *The Australian*, 15 September 1981.

2. *National Times*, 13-19 September 1981, p. 1.

3. Ibid., p. 8.

4. Norman Abjorensen, "Leadership in the Liberal Party: Bolte, Askin and the Post-War Ascendancy," PhD thesis, Faculty of Arts, The Australian National University, December 2004, p. 19.

5. Ian Hancock, "Askin, Robin," p. 347.

6. Ian Hancock, "Askin, Robin," p. 348; NSW Registry of Births Deaths and Marriages, History of the Registry's Records, http://www.bdm.nsw.gov.au/familyHistory/historyRecords.htm, Accessed on 17 August 2008, p. 3.

7. Shurlee Swain and Renee Howe, *Single Mothers and Their Children: Disposal, Punishment and Survival in Australia*, Cambridge University Press, Cambridge, 1999, p. 180.

8. Ibid., p. 195.

9. Interview (Mel Pratt): Sir Robert Askin, 1976, National Library of Australia, ORAL, TRC 121/83, 1:1/1-2.

10. Freda MacDonnell, *The Glebe: Portraits and Places*, Ure Smith, Sydney, 1976, p. 113.

11. MacDonnell, *The Glebe*, p. 113.

12. Ibid.

13. Interview (Pratt): Sir Robert Askin, 1:1/1-2.

14. MacDonnell, *The Glebe*, p. 113.

15. Abjorensen, "Leadership in the Liberal Party," p. 216.

16. Alan Barcan, *Two Centuries of Education in New South Wales*, University of New South Wales Press, Sydney, 1988. p. 189.

17. *Sydney Technical High School Journal*, Volume I, May 1916, p. 8.

18. *Sydney Technical High School Year Book*, 1969, p. 56.

19. MacDonnell, *The Glebe*, p. 113.

20. Interview (Pratt): Sir Robert Askin, 1:1/4.

21 Frank Cain, *Jack Lang and the Great Depression*, Australian Scholarly, Melbourne, 2005, p. 183.

22 Interview (Pratt): Sir Robert Askin, 1:1/4.

23 Murray Goot, "Askin, Sir Robert (Robin) William," in *Australian Dictionary of Bibliography*, Vol.17, Melbourne University Press, Melbourne, p. 36.

24 NSW Births, Deaths and Marriages, Marriage certificate 1937/ 005002.

25 Interview (Pratt): Sir Robert Askin, 1:1/11.

26 Geoffrey Reading, *High Climbers: Askin and Others*, John Ferguson, Sydney, 1989, p. 17.

27 Interview (Pratt): Sir Robert Askin, 1:1/18.

28 AIF Service Record, B883 / 2002 / 04608381 / NX93958.

29 Interview (Pratt): Sir Robert Askin, 1:1/19.

30 Ibid.

31 Hancock, "Askin, Robin," p. 350.

32 Ibid.

33 Abjorensen, "Leadership in the Liberal Party," p. 225.

34 Katharine West, *Power in the Liberal Party: A Study in Australian Politics*, Cheshire, Melbourne, 1965, p. 152.

35 *NSW Parliamentary Debates (PD) Legislative Assembly (LA), Series 3,* Vol. 2, p.1282 and p. 1415.

36 Interview (Paul Loughnan) with Graeme Starr, 5 July 2020.

37 NSW *PD, LA,* 1 September 1954, p. 140.

38 *Sunday Telegraph*, 28 January 1962.

39 LPA ML MSS 2385 K53642 Item 10.

40 Joel Bateman, "The Loss of Leadership – Machiavelli and Australian Prime Ministers," PhD thesis, School of Political Science and International Studies, University of Queensland, October 2006, p. 8.

41 Norman Abjorensen, "Thomas Lancelot Lewis," in David Clune and Ken Turner, (eds), *The Premiers of New South Wales, Volume 2, 1901-2005*, Federation Press, Sydney, 2006, p. 377.

42 Ibid.

43 *Sydney Morning Herald (SMH)*, 22 October 1971.

44 Robert Parker, *The Government of New South Wales*, University

of Queensland Press, St. Lucia, 1978, p. 435.

45 Interview (Paul Loughnan) with the Hon. Wallace (Wal) Clyde Fife, 10 July 2009.

46 Wal Fife, *A Country Liberal*, Wallace Clyde Fife, Wagga Wagga, 2008, p. 106.

47 Interview (Paul Loughnan) with Sir John Fuller, 10 January 2008.

48 Interview (Paul Loughnan) with The Hon. Milton Arthur Morris, AO, 20 August 2009.

49 Interview (Loughnan) with Starr.

50 Paul Davey, "Charles Cutler: A lesson in Coalition partnership with Premier Askin," in Ken Turner and Michael Hogan, (eds), *The Worldly Art of Politics*, Federation Press, Sydney, 2006, p. 175.

51 Abjorensen, "Leadership in the Liberal Party," p. 278.

52 Interview (Loughnan) with Fuller.

53 Ian Hancock, *The Liberals: A History of the NSW Division of the Liberal Party of Australia 1945-2000*, Federation Press, Sydney, 2007, p. 111.

54 Interview (Loughnan) with Starr.

55 *SMH,* 2 June 1965.

56 *Cabinet Papers*, 4 June 1965. SUBJECT: Report of Premiers' Conference and meeting of Loan Council. Decision: Premiers comments and the decision of the Cabinet.

57 *SMH*, 18 June 1966.

58 Hancock, "Askin, Robin," p.357 (ref *NSWPD* 15 August 1968, p.269.)

59 *SMH,* 11 February 1972; *SMH,* 12 February 1972.

60 Gough Whitlam, *The Whitlam Government: 1972-1975*, Penguin, Ringwood,1985, p. 386; *SMH*, 23 August 1973.

61 *SMH*, 15 July 1964.

62 Graeme Starr, *Variety and Choice: Good Schools for All Australians*, Menzies Research Centre, Canberra, 2010, p. 48; Graeme Starr, *Carrick: Principles, Politics and Policy*, Connor Court Publishing, Ballan, 2012, p. 171.

63 Dempsey, "1968," *The People's Choice*, p. 4.

64 Malcolm Mackerras, *New South Wales Elections*, Australian

National University, Canberra, 1973, p. 178, 181.
65 Interview (Loughnan) with Starr.
66 *The Bulletin*, 5 June 1965, p. 19.
67 *SMH*, 30 April 1965.
68 *The Bulletin*, 5 June 1965, p. 19.
69 "Australian Political Chronicle January-April 1968," *Australian Journal of Politics and History (AJPH)*, Vol.14, No.2, p. 246.
70 *SMH*, 19 February 1968.
71 *The Bulletin*, 27 October 1973, p.14; *The Daily Telegraph*, 21 June 1973; *The Daily Telegraph*, 17 November 1973.
72 *Australian Financial Review (AFR)*, 3 October 1973.
73 *The Australian*, 19 November 1973.
74 'Go Go' girls were professional dancers, who performed on musical variety television shows such as Bandstand when the art form was fashionable in the 1960s and early 1970s.
75 *The Australian*, 19 November 1973.
76 Fife, *A Country Liberal*, p. 107.
77 *SMH*, 14-15 October 2006.
78 *Daily Telegraph*, 18 October 1966.
79 Ibid., 22 October 1966.
80 *The Sun*, 21 October 1966.
81 *Daily Telegraph*, 14 October 1966.
82 *SMH*, 15 October 1966.
83 Ibid., 10 October 1966.
84 *Daily Telegraph*, 15 October 1966; *SMH*, 15 October 1966.
85 *SMH*, 19 October 1966; *The Sun*, 21 October 1966; *The Sun*, 25 October 1966; *Daily Mirror*, 21 October 1966.
86 *The Bulletin*, 29 October 1966, p. 8; *The Sun*, 24 October 1966.
87 *SMH*, 23 October 1966.
88 *The Bulletin*, 29 October 1966, p. 8; *Daily Mirror* 22 October 1966.
89 *Daily Mirror,* 22 October 1966.
90 *SMH*, 23 October 1966.
91 Ibid.
92 *Daily Telegraph*, 22 October 1966; *Daily Telegraph*, 24 October

1966.

93 *SMH*, 23 October 1966; *SMH*, 24 October 1966; *Daily Telegraph*, 24 October 1966.

94 *The Sun*, 24 October 1966; *The Sun*, 22 October 1966; *Daily Mirror*, 22 October 1966; *The Australian*, 24 October 1966.

95 *SMH*, 23 October 1966; *SMH*, 21 October 1966.

96 *The Sun* 20 October 1966 *Daily Telegraph*, 20 October 1966; *The Australian*, 20 October 1966; *SMH*, 29 October 1966.

97 *The Australian*, 24 October 1966.

98 *Daily Telegraph*, 24 October 1966.

99 *The Bulletin*, 22 September 1981, p. 32.

100 *SMH*, 24 July 1968.

101 Interview (Mel Pratt): Sir Robert Askin, 1976, National Library of Australia, ORAL, TRC 121/83, 1:2/27

102 Jack Mundey, *Green Bans and Beyond*, Angus and Robertson, North Ryde, 1981, p. 82.

103 Hancock, "Askin, Robin," p. 369, Peter Spearritt, *Sydney Since the Twenties*, Hale and Iremonger, Sydney, 1978, p. 108.

104 *National Times*, 13-19 September 1981, p. 1.

105 Alfred McCoy, *Drug Traffic: Narcotics and Organized Crime in Australia*, Harper and Row, Sydney, 1980, p. 97,103.

106 Athol Moffitt, *A Quarter to Midnight: The Australian Crisis, Organised Crime and the Decline of the Institutions of State*, Angus and Robertson, North Ryde, 1985, p. 11, 66

107 McCoy, *Drug Traffic*, p.72.

108 Several of these were initiated by the Commonwealth and were supported by NSW and most of the other states.

109 Moffitt, *A Quarter to Midnight*, p. 70.

110 Ibid., p. 150.

111 Ibid., p. 237.

112 Ibid., p. 236.

113 In a telephone interview with the author, Souter confirmed that the contents of the book were sanctioned by the Fairfax board.

114 David Hickie, *The Prince and the Premier*, Angus and Robertson, North Ryde, 1985, p. 59.

115 *SMH*, 28 November 1993; Interview (Paul Loughnan) with David Hickie, 30 April 2012.

116 *National Times*, September 13 - 19, 1981, p. 1.

117 Ibid., p. 8.

118 *National Times*, 4-10 January 1981, p. 1.

119 Hickie, *The Prince and the Premier*, p. 20.

120 Ibid., p. 11.

121 Ibid., p. 20.

122 Evan Whitton, *Can of Worms: A Citizen's Reference Book to Crime and the Administration of Justice*, Fairfax Library, Broadway, 1986, pp. 328-329.

123 Tony Reeves, *Mr Sin: The Abe Saffron Dossier*, Allen and Unwin, Sydney 2007, p. I ; Committee on the Office of the Ombudsman and the Police Integrity Commission, *Research Report on Trends in Police Corruption*, NSW Parliament, December 2002, p. 26.

124 Reeves, *Mr Sin*, p.6.

125 *SMH*, 15 January 2010.

126 G.P. Walsh, "Freeman, George David (1935–1990)," Australian Dictionary of Biography, http://adb.anu.edu.au/ accessed 3 July 2012; Hickie, *The Prince and the Premier*, p. 88.

127 Bob Bottom, *Connections: Crime, Rackets, and Networks of Influence Down-under*, Sun Books, Sydney, 1985, p. 119; Whitton, *Can of Worms*, pp. 280-283.

128 Gavin Souter, *Heralds and Angels – The House of Fairfax*, Penguin Books, Sydney, 1990, p. 145.

129 Ibid., p.147.

130 Ibid., p.148.

131 Souter, *Heralds and Angels*, p. 145.

132 *National Times*, 4-10 January 1981, p. 12.

133 Ibid.

134 Ibid., p. 14.

135 *National Times*, 4-10 January 1981, p. 13.

136 Ibid., p. 14.

137 Ibid., p. 12.

138 Hickie, *The Prince and the Premier*, p. 374; Reeves, *Mr Sin*, p. viii.

139 *The Australian* 20 June 1973; *The Australian*, 19 June 1973; *The Australian*, 17 August 1973; *The Sun*, 18 June 1973.

140 *National Times*, 4-10 January 1981, p. 12; Committee on the Office of the Ombudsman and the Police Integrity Commission, *Research Report on Trends in Police Corruption*, p. 23.

141 Souter, *Heralds and Angels*, p. 149; *SMH*, 14-15 July 2012.

142 'Deep Throat' was the alias given to the impeccable source whose evidence helped impeach US President Nixon – Carl Bernstein and Bob Woodward, *All the President's Men*, Simon and Schuster, New York, 1974, p .71.

143 *National Times*, 13-19 September 1981, p. 1, 8.

144 Souter, *Heralds and Angels*, pp. 145-146.

145 *National Times*, 13-19 September 1981, p. 1.

146 *National Times*, 13-19 September 1981, p. 1.

147 Ibid.

148 Ibid., p. 8.

149 This was established by the Commonwealth Government along with the New South Wales, Queensland and Victorian governments.

150 Whitton, *Can of Worms*, pp. 44-46, 337.

151 *The Bulletin*, 15 September 1981, p. 15, 83.

152 *National Times*, 20-26 September 1981, p. 3.

153 Hancock, "Askin, Robin," p. 365.

154 Ibid., p. 366.

155 *The Sun*, 16 September 1981; *National Times*, 20-26 September 1981, p. 9.

156 *National Times*, 20-26 September 1981, p. 9.

157 *Daily Telegraph*, 14 September 1981; *National Times*, 20-26 September 1981, p. 9.

158 *Daily Mirror*, 14 September 1981; *National Times*, 20-26 September 1981, p. 9.

159 Souter, *Heralds and Angels*, p. 144.

160 Ibid., p. 146.

161 Ibid.

162 Reading, *High Climbers: Askin and Others*, p. 142.

163 Ibid., p. 144.

164 Souter, *Heralds and Angels,* p. 146.
165 Ibid., p. 147.
166 *National Times*, 27 September to 3 October 1981, p. 1.
167 Souter, *Heralds and Angels,* p. 147.
168 Ibid.
169 Hancock, "Askin, Robin," p. 365.
170 Souter, *Heralds and Angels,* p. 146.
171 *National Times,* 29 March – 4 April 1985, p. 25.
172 Ibid.
173 Ibid.
174 *National Times,* p. 25.
175 *Sun Herald*, 31 March 1985.
176 *The Sun, 28* March 1985.
177 *Sunday Telegraph,* 31 March 1985.
178 *Daily Mirror*, 28 March 1985.
179 *Daily Telegraph,* 28 March 1985.
180 Ibid.
181 *The Australian*, 28 March 1985; *Daily Telegraph,* 28 March 1985.
182 *The Sun*, 28 March 1985; *Daily Mirror*, 28 March 1985.
183 *NSW PD, LA,* 28 March 1985, pp. 5361-5363.
184 *Sunday Telegraph*, 31 March 1985.
185 *SMH*,14 June 1985.
186 *Sun Herald*, 31 March 1985.
187 *Sun Herald*, 31 March 1985.
188 *The Sun,* 13 November 1986.
189 Bob Bottom, signed statement provided to the author, dated 28 May 2012.
190 *SMH*, 31 March 1987.
191 Inquiry into the Establishment and Operation of Legal Casinos in New South Wales, NSW Government, Sydney, 1991.
192 Ibid., 4 December 1991.
193 Ibid., 12 June 1993.
194 *The National Times,* 13-19 September 1981, p.1, 8.

195 Interview (Paul Loughnan) with Bob Bottom, 26 May 2012.
196 Ibid.
197 Ibid.
198 Interview (Paul Loughnan) with the Hon. Jim Carlton AO, 5 December 2008.
199 Abjorensen, "Leadership in the Liberal Party," p. 292; *The Bulletin*, 1 July 1986.
200 An article presenting the "Waller report" was published in the *SMH* on 28 November 1993; a fully copy of the original 8-page report is in the possession of the author of this monograph.
201 *SMH*, "Median Sydney property price movements 1965-1980," extract from "BIS Shrapnel" report, 12 August 1981.
202 Standard and Poors, *Australian Share Price Movements*, Sydney, November 2009, p. 1.
203 Waller Report.
204 Interview (Loughnan) with Starr.
205 Waller Report
206 Hickie, *The Prince and the Premier*, p. 84.
207 *Sun Herald*, 28 November 1993.
208 Annelise Anderson, *The Business of Organised Crime: A Cosa Nostra Family*, Hoover Institution Press, Stanford, 1979, p. 76; Michael D. Maltz, "Defining Organised Crime," in Robert J. Kelly, Ko-Lin Chin and Rufus Schatzberg, (eds), *Handbook of Organized Crime in the United States*, Greenwood Press, Westport, 1994, p. 27.
209 Hickie, *The Prince and the Premier*, p. 19.
210 Ibid., pp. 376-378.
211 *SMH*, 25 March 1985.
212 Anderson, *The Business of Organised Crime*, p. 76; Hickie, *The Prince and the Premier*, p. 376; *SMH*, 25 March 1985, pp. 6-7.
213 Reeves, *Mr Sin*, p. vii.
214 Robert Kelly and Rufus Schatzberg, "'Once upon a time in America' – Organised crime and civil society" in Felia Allum and Renate Siebert (eds), *Organised Crime and the Challenge to Democracy*, Routledge, London, 2003, p. 137.
215 Anderson, *The Business of Organised Crime*, p. 78.

216 Kelly and Schatzberg, "Organised crime and civil society," p. 137.

217 Anderson, *The Business of Organised Crime*, p. 79; United Nations Office on Drugs and Crime, *An Assessment of Transnational Organized Crime in Central Asia*, New York, 2006, p .44.

218 Kelly and Schatzberg, "Organised crime and civil society," p. 137; Anderson, *The Business of Organised Crime*, p. 79.

219 *SMH*, 4 July 1993.

220 *The Australian*, 10 October 1973; *SMH*, 16 June 1973.

221 *SMH*, 13 August 1974.

222 *NSW PD, LA*, 27 August 1974, p. 647.

223 *NSW PD, LA*, 27 August 1974, p. 647.

224 Bob Bottom, *The Godfather in Australia: Organised Crime's Australian Connections*, Reed, Sydney, 1979, p. 103.

225 Ibid.

226 Ibid., p. 110.

227 Ibid., p.107.

228 Ibid., p.108,110.

229 Bottom, *The Godfather in Australia*, pp. 109-110.

230 Whitton, *Can of Worms*, p. 16; Moffitt, *A Quarter to Midnight*, p. 72; Bob Bottom, *Without Fear or Favour*, Sun Books, South Melbourne, 1984. pp. 30-31.

231 Moffitt, *A Quarter to Midnight*, p. 72.

232 Moffitt, *A Quarter to Midnight*, p. 72.

233 *The Australian*, 17 August 1973.

234 *The Sun*, 20 August 1973.

235 *Daily Telegraph*, 23 March 1974.

236 Bottom, *Without Fear or Favour*, pp. 34-35.

237 Ibid.

238 *Daily Telegraph*, 15 August 1974.

239 *The Australian*, 15 August 1974; Athol Moffitt, (Chair), Royal Commission into Organised Crime in Registered Clubs, *Report*, New South Wales Government Printer, Sydney, 1974, pp. 134-135; *Daily Telegraph*, 15 August 1974.

240 *NSW PD LA*, 20 August 1974, pp. 431-432.

241 *NSW PD LA*, 4 December 1973, p. 27.
242 Waller Report.
243 Murray Goot, "Askin, Sir Robert William (Bob) (1907–1981)," Australian Dictionary of Biography, http://adb.anu.edu.au/ accessed 29 July 2012.
244 Waller Report.
245 *The Australian,* 14 May 1974.
246 Stuart Littlemore, ABC Media Watch, 4 October 1993.
247 Interviews (Loughnan) with Fife, Morris and Fuller.
248 Interview (Paul Loughnan) with John Hatton AO, 19 May 2012; Reading, *High Climbers*, p. 142.
249 Hancock, "Askin, Robin," p.3 66.
250 *SMH*, 31 July 2018.
251 *The Manly Daily*, 16 Sept 1981.
252 Hickie, *The Prince and the Premier*, p. 88.
253 https://www.acnc.gov.au/charity
254 Norman Abjorensen, "Leadership in the Liberal Party," p. 19.
255 Ian Hancock, "Askin, Robin," p. 347.
256 https://www.acnc.gov.au/charity
257 Email to author from David Marr via his publisher Black Inc. on 31 May 2012.

www.ingramcontent.com/pod-product-compliance
Lightning Source LLC
Chambersburg PA
CBHW071626170426
43195CB00038B/2148